LAMPPOSTS
Letters to the Grieving

Moving Through Loss and
Disappointment to Healing and Hope

By KATIE LUSE

Lampposts, Letters to the Grieving
© Copyright 2022 by Katie Luse

All Rights Reserved. No part of *Lampposts, Letters to the Grieving* may be reproduced, stored in a retrieval system, or transmitted, in any form or by any means—by electronic, mechanical, photocopying, recording or otherwise—in any form without permission. Thank you for buying an authorized edition of this book and for complying with copyright laws.

Scriptures marked NIV are taken from the NEW INTERNATIONAL VERSION (NIV): Scripture taken from THE HOLY BIBLE, NEW INTERNATIONAL VERSION ®. Copyright© 1973, 1978, 1984, 2011 by Biblica, Inc.TM. Used by permission of Zondervan

Scriptures marked NKJV are taken from the NEW KING JAMES VERSION (NKJV): Scripture taken from the NEW KING JAMES VERSION®. Copyright© 1982 by Thomas Nelson, Inc. Used by permission. All rights reserved.

Scriptures marked ESV are taken from the THE HOLY BIBLE, ENGLISH STANDARD VERSION (ESV): Scriptures taken from THE HOLY BIBLE, ENGLISH STANDARD VERSION ® Copyright© 2001 by Crossway, a publishing ministry of Good News Publishers. Used by permission.

Scripture quotations taken from the (NASB®) New American Standard Bible®, Copyright © 1960, 1971, 1977, 1995, 2020 by The Lockman Foundation. Used by permission. All rights reserved.

Scripture quotations marked (GNB) are taken from the GOOD NEWS BIBLE© 1994 published by the Bible Societies/HarperCollins Publishers Ltd UK, Good News Bible© American Bible Society 1966, 1971, 1976, 1992. Used with permission.

Scripture quotations marked (BCB) are taken from The Holy Bible, Berean Study Bible, BSB Copyright ©2016, 2020 by Bible Hub. Used by Permission. All Rights Reserved Worldwide.

Edited by Susan Thompson
Cover Design by Kristen Ingebretson
Proofread by Jennifer Cullis, Printopya LLC
Interior Design by A. Banales, Printopya LLC
Headshot Photo by Natalie Zigarovich

Published by Luse Productions, LLC
www.katieluse.com

Paperback ISBN: 979-8-9864243-0-9
eISBN: 979-8-9864243-1-6

First Edition

Printed in the United States.

TO THE GRIEVING

You are the heroes of our world. You are brave. You can do this. It will not always be this dark, and you will not always feel this sad. Night doesn't come after night. Morning will break, and you will feel joy again.

Just get to the next plot of light.

TABLE OF CONTENTS

Introduction ix
How to Read This Book xiii
Part 1: Entering In 1
    Permission to Grieve 2
    Your Heart Matters 5
    Proximity to God 6
    Grief Can Be Trusted 7
    Shores of Grace 8
Part 2: Honoring Your Grief 9
    Your Pain Matters 10
    Take the Hand of Grief 11
    Feeling Invisible 12
    Thawing Out 13
    Enforcing Space 14
    Weighed Down 15
    Something to Hold 16
    Sudden Motivation 17
    Irritability 18

Friendships 20
The Trap of Busyness 22
Be Still 23

Part 3: Making Decisions 25
Aids and Detriments 26
Burial 27
Your Pace, Your Process 29
Throwing Things Away 31
Be Careful with Your Story 32
Holidays 34
To Those Who Grieve on Christmas 35
Using Names 37
Protecting Your Beliefs 38

Part 4: Staying Healthy 41
Getting Your Needs Met 42
Personal Hygiene 43
Anger 44
Sleep 46
Physical Symptoms 47
Seeing Past Yourself 49
Negativity 50
Comfort Food 51
Building Walls 52
Serving Others 54
The Need for Nature 55
Celebrate Each Step 57

Part 5: Exerting Courage 59
Moving Forward 60
Coming Out of Hiding 62
That Same Old Feeling 63
Embracing Change 64
Social Settings 65

  Facing Another Day 67
  Reentry 68
  Reasons to Continue 69
  Seasons Will Change 70
  Courage to Trust Again 72

Part 6: Pacing Your Process 75
  Permission to Be Happy 76
  Catapulted Backward 78
  Gentleness 79
  Making Ongoing Memories 80
  Giving Up 81
  Short-term Memories 82
  Two Steps Forward, One Step Back 83
  Walk Away 84

Part 7: Leaning on God 85
  Prayer 86
  The Helper 87
  Refined in the Fire 88
  Questions for God 89
  When Everything Fails 90
  Your Role and God's Role 91
  Moving On 92
  Loneliness 93

Part 8: Embracing Reality 95
  Waiting for Reality to Repent 96
  Looking for the Exit 97
  People Can't Solve This 98
  Regrets 99
  Self-perception 100
  Moving Out of Blame 101
  Closure 102
  Does This Last Forever? 103

Part 9: Releasing Your Grip **105**
    Letting Your Heart Go Free 106
    When Grief Resigns 108
    A Lot to Unlearn 110
    The Imprint of Loss 111

Part 10: Redemption Bells **113**
    Early Stages 114
    Trusting God's Artistry 116
    A Call out of Apathetic Hope 117
    Redeemer God 119
    Until Your Heart Is Full Again 120
    When Redemption Comes 122
    Justice 123
    The Value of Time 124
    Extensions into Eternity 127
    The Bells of Redemption 129

Thank You **133**
Tell Your Story **135**

INTRODUCTION

A few months after my daughter, Ruby Joy, died of a genetic disease, a friend said to me, "You should write a book on grief." I took the paper that was in my hand and crumpled it up fiercely until I was holding it as tightly as a disheveled ball. I then opened it back up, tore it into pieces, and threw it away. "That," I answered, "is what a book on grief would look like."

I have long believed that a book on grief would need to have missing pages, crumpled pages, pages that were scribbled on with a black permanent marker bleeding unapologetically forward. It would need torn pages, pages upside down, pages in unknown languages, pages of explicit language, pages of angry art, and pages that are prickly to the touch, like a cactus. "Anyone who thinks they can write a book on grief has no idea what grief is." That was *my* confident response to my poor friend who could see much more clearly than I where my own journey was headed.

I am still of the conviction that any linear depiction of grief is an injustice to what it is. The perfunctory chapter outlines on how to navigate loss disturb me. I am the person standing in the bookstore's grief section in utter despair at what is missing. Science cannot solve these seasons of our lives. There is no psychological, spiritual, mental, or emotional formula for this process that is universal.

Many of my grief writings are terribly depressing, littered with bad language, and pulsing with disturbing sorrow. I remember a drawing that I did of tangled yarn, knotted and hopelessly twisted. I wrote a caption for it, "Dear Katie, Unravel this. –Grief."

I do not feel the need to publish all of these expressions; however, I do feel the need to publish something. Those who are grieving need a voice, a voice that attempts to understand, a voice that heralds this muted and yet universal experience in our culture, a voice that champions this holy experience that can produce gold inside of humankind.

I am daring to be that voice. Herein lies my book on grief. It is not exhaustive. It is not conclusive. It is not orderly. No sooner could I pin down the wind than a universal grief process. We all grieve differently, but we also all grieve.

In the last few years I discovered that the world is grieving. We are all grieving something. This grief can be anything from the loss of a loved one to a recent move. For some it is the trauma of lack in an area of their lives, a disappointment experienced, a transition that yields unexpected results. Some grieve when nothing changes; others grieve when things change. Some are catapulted into deep grief that we trumpet as "a tragedy," while still others silently grieve the tragedy of what they never had. Whatever the cause of grief, it is always a process that holds commonalities for all of us. Those commonalties are what I am attempting to capture in this book. At least some of them.

This book is written foremost for the grieving, offering "lampposts" of understanding. My hope is that the grieving will find themselves personally in these letters, and therein gain understanding and purpose where they otherwise would have found disorientation and confusion. This book is also written for those who want to love well someone who is grieving, because many people are at a loss on how to relate to those who grieve. These writings give voice to the grief process and offer understanding to anyone who seeks it.

>For the darkness that I also know.
>Take courage.
>You are not alone.
>
>Here are some *letters to the grieving*.
>Letters to you.
>Lampposts for the journey.

With love,

Katie Luse

HOW TO READ THIS BOOK

This book is not designed to be read in order but rather read like a pile of letters. Pick one up, put it back down. Pick up another, put it back down. The order is your choice. Perhaps the titles will draw you to the right one at the right time, or perhaps God will do that. He always does it best. Or perhaps you will read the whole thing in order and find a rhythm there that is just what you need.

Keep the book as long as you need it. Write in it. Respond to it. Interact with it. Let it feed you however it can. And take your time. Grief does not get along well with clocks.

The grief process can feel mysterious and is not something we ask for. I will do my best to lead you gently in these pages and therein help you discover rather than explode upon grief's realities. You have the strength to get through this; you can do this.

Part 1: Entering In

Permission to Grieve

I lost my daughter to a terminal disease. She was two years and eight months old when she went Home. I am a mom. I live with loss. Early in my grief journey a trusted friend looked me straight in the eye and said, "I am so sorry, Katie, but you cannot run from this. You must go *through* it."

Weird idea. Who wants to embrace pain?

No one. But when you discover that the deepest love, most profound comfort, and invaluable teaching happen in the crux of pain, you stop fearing it.

I remember a moment in particular when I was at a meeting and felt the sorrow of grief rising in my heart. Instead of pushing it back down, I sat on the floor and cried for a long time. Deep expression tumbled out of my broken heart. I let the tears fall and fall hard. I wept and didn't try to stop it. I gripped the sense of the Holy Spirit's hand in mine and poured out my heart without reservation. I was a mess on the floor in a public space and did not care because I have learned that my heart honestly expressed is of value to Father God.

Three hours later a series of events occurred that caused me to feel a height of joy that was brand new. It was so encouraging that it took me off guard. It wasn't long before I realized that the joy that ambushed me was connected to my tears that had just hit the floor. Joy was coming as a response.

Consider...

> *Blessed are those who mourn, for they will be comforted.*
> —*Matthew 5:4, NIV*

> *...weeping may stay for the night, but rejoicing comes in the morning.*
> —*Psalm 30:5, NIV*

> *To comfort all who mourn, and to provide for those who grieve in Zion—to bestow on them a crown of beauty instead of ashes, the oil of joy instead of mourning, and a garment of praise instead of a spirit of despair.*
>
> —Isaiah 61:2-3, NIV

Have you ever noticed that these scriptures are allocated *specifically* to those who grieve? These outcomes and rewards are for those who embrace the hard work of grief and let it happen. What if weeping is a passageway to joy? What if mourning sets the stage for comfort? What if ashes are the prime materials needed to create beauty? What if resistance to grief revokes its provisions?

People get over stuff all the time without healing from it. I believe that healing happens when we courageously face the reality of our pain and encounter who God is for us in our grief. Friends, it is in the tears, the groans, the raw outpouring of our hearts before God that we encounter the God who heals.

God attaches provision to grief, which is why it is not okay to deny each other access to it. There's something about the freedom to weep, mourn, and grieve that sets the stage for joy, comfort, and beauty. Too often people fear what they cannot fix and therefore short-circuit someone else's grief process because of their own discomfort with it. In that lack of permission, we also resist the God-given provisions to those who grieve.

I can't fix your hurt, but I can tell you that it matters to God. In that validation, I hope your hands will be untied to face what you feel and then pour your heart out to Him.

Grief is not a dead end.

It will lead you to something.

Weeping, mourning, and grieving will lead you to…

...comfort, joy, beauty, and praise. (See Matthew 5:4; Psalm 30:5; Isaiah 61:2-3.)

Give yourself permission to grieve.

> *Trust in him at all times, you people; pour out your hearts to him; for God is our refuge.*
>
> —*Psalm 62:8, NIV*

Your Heart Matters

I want you to know that despite its beastly appearances, grief is not your enemy right now. Grief is actually a God-given mechanism for processing pain. It can be the giver of a beautiful journey through a terrible time, a road that validates the needs of your heart as you navigate this season. Your heart matters, and grief gives your heart a voice.

Grief is an epic trek through an invisible world. It will lead you into unforeseen places, connect you with new people, teach you about life beneath the surface, and test the strength of your heart, most thoroughly. It will carve out a depth of your soul that you would never ask for, nor ever trade. Grief gives you its process. It is incremental and can be gentle.

Every once in a while, you will encounter someone who sees you in grief and somehow knows it without your pleading explanations. These brief moments of companionship are a baptism of fresh air, a validation that the madness of your unseen internal life is both real and beautiful. But this companionship can be hard to find. It is a foreign language to those whom it has not yet arrested by its deep love.

Grief is holy and terrible, a gift and a tragedy. It is a friend and an enemy, gentle and beastly. It is weird and synchronized, mysterious and plain. Grief is not easily tied down and defined. And yet to some, it is most familiar.

I, for one.
You, for another.
We, together.
Grief is the sound of love.
Your love.
And, at times it is a friend.

Proximity to God

Friendship with the Holy Spirit is the paramount aid in grief. He is a counselor like none other. I do not recommend navigating grief without the support of an active relationship with God. He will love you in a way that no one else can right now. If you do not currently have a relationship with God, it is time to start one. No matter who you are, or what you've done, Jesus is calling. Come home.

Jesus, I give my life to you today. Be my Lord, be my Friend, be my Counselor. I surrender to you. I need you.

That said, proximity to God is your choice. As one who grieves, you can choose to run into God or away from Him with your pain. He will love you with the same undying love no matter what you choose. He will always be there for you if you run away and come back. And He will be able to support you much better if your arms remain open to His by choice every day of this process. Run in. Choose to run into God.

Grief Can Be Trusted

Grief is like a cloud. It hazes your visibility, darkens your scene, and slows your pace. But it also guides you through the storm, shields you from the scorching sun, and dissolves itself in time. Grief can be trusted, and when trusted, it does its best and quickest work.

I have never known greater intimacy with God than those times of meeting Him in the crux of grief. He will meet you in the darkness. He will guide you with a cloud. The amputation you have is an invitation for the broken body and poured out blood of Christ to be sewn into the fabric of your deepest being so that at last you become one with Christ.

It is here in the storm that you will find out who you are, who God is, and that you are never alone. In your own collision with these truths, grief will liberate you from bondages you long lived with. Many fears in your life will breathe their last and die. Your walk through your grief can set you free.

Left to one holy solution, grief is an invitation to intimacy with God that will reshape your life into one of simple devotion. As fire is to gold, so grief is to love.

> Your Maker is in love with you.
> Your time in the cloud will teach you that.
> That, and so much more.
>
> If you dare to enter in.
>
> Do not fear, beloved.
> God is here.

The people remained at a distance, while Moses approached the thick darkness where God was.

—*Exodus 20:21, NIV*

Shores of Grace

The ocean's waves hit the shoreline over and over again, yet the tide is a mystery to those who have never studied it. Millions of people stare at the tide daily, but few understand its ways. If you approach the shore uninformed, you can become a victim to whatever the water happens to be doing at that time.

Those who take the time to research the ways of water and the tides understand that there are known patterns. With this understanding comes the knowledge to know whether to dive in for enjoyment or run away for safety prior to contact. For those whose livelihood depends on the water, understanding is crucial.

So too it is with grief.

When you understand the process of grieving, you can better navigate the shores of loss in a way that enables the greatest enjoyment of grief's beauty and the fiercest protection from its threats.

Welcome to the shores of loss that couple as the shores of grace.

They are not all stormy. Some are immensely beautiful.

We can learn about them here together.

Unafraid.

Part 2: Honoring Your Grief

Your Pain Matters

If this moment of your life were on a whiteboard, I would aggressively erase it as fast as I could. I would take this blotchy, terrible reality you are facing and turn it back into a pure white board. I would wake you up and tell you that it was only a dream. Or shoot the loss down until it let you go free. I am so sorry for your loss.

> It is not fair.
> It is not right.
>
> It is unwelcomed.
> I scream with you.
> I weep with you.
> I resist with you.
> Your pain matters.

Take the Hand of Grief

You grieve because you love.

Don't let anyone talk you out of your grief. Or accuse you in it. Your love needs an outlet, and that outlet right now is grief. If you did not love, you would not grieve. Your grief will exist as an entity of its own. It will sometimes feel like a part of you and other times more outside of you. You must begin to see that grief is actually for you.

Honor your grief. It is a mysterious thing, a God-given processing tool for emotional pain. Grief is effective. It heals. Moving *through* grief is the quickest way to safety for your heart. Dodging its presentations is nothing more than the pocketing of pain for another time.

When you learn to take the hand of grief, you will find that there is strategy to its seeming madness. It will gift you with one provision after another as you navigate your loss.

Grief.

Hold its hand.

Trust it.

Honor it.

Feeling Invisible

Your loss is like an amputation. Something is gone and it left behind a blaringly obvious gap in your life. Because it is an amputation of the heart and soul, your grief is not always visible to others. You feel it steadily though, as a certain marker on yourself.

While interacting with certain people, you will realize that they can't see your grief. This is hard to believe because your pain could not deny itself with the best intentions. Your amputation is as real as your name right now.

It takes a height of maturity to maintain an interaction with someone who does not acknowledge your pain without you hijacking the conversation to give grief a voice. You want to shake the person. "Do you not see me?" cries your heart. Yet, a hijack may cost you more than you think. There is no guarantee that the person will care for your pain well, even when made aware of it.

Instead of becoming your pain's advocate, in those moments when you feel invisible to others, become more aware of how the Father sees you and how much He cares about you. To Him you are visible, even highlighted. The more revelation you gain about this, the more your amputation will lose its ache for a voice and instead become steadily held by the Father, where it is safe.

God sees you.

Cast all your anxiety on him because he cares for you.
—1 Peter 5:7, NIV

Thawing Out

As you move through your grieving process, you thaw out slowly to reality. It is like the melting of a gigantic piece of ice with bad news inside. The people around you seem to be making more headway in embracing this reality than you. You stare at them in disbelief at times as they mention facts about your loss that you still cannot believe. Your ability to process your loss is more challenging for you than for anyone else because it impacts you the most. You cannot seem to get a grip on its reality.

I think this "thawing out to reality" is a psychological grace. It may feel disorienting to watch others respond to facts about you that you have yet to assimilate, but your heart can only take so much each day, and that is okay. Embrace the process and don't feel the need to thrash the giant piece of ice against stones until it tells you the truth. The truth is already with you. No need to rush its invasion.

There are times when you feel like nothing happened, that the loss is not real. This is okay. Give yourself permission in those times to make some headway on a vision for your future. There are other times when the loss will feel too real, as if it is the only thing that is still real. That is okay too. It will not own your world for long.

Thawing out to reality is one of those areas where grief will do the hard work for you if you let it. Whatever your moment is, and however it lends itself to how you process reality in that moment, you *can* be present in it.

Let yourself thaw out, and let it take time.

Grace is in reality.

Enforcing Space

Sometimes you need space from your grief. Give yourself permission to choose to walk away from the hard work of your loss. Ignore it for a minute.

Are you really not visiting the grave on his/her birthday?

Are you really not mentioning his/her name right now?

Are you really not correcting that person on their misconceptions about grief?

Are you really not taking the opportunity to memorialize right now?

No, I am really not.

Permission. Have grace for yourself. The inability to face something at its core is a sign of how deep your love is running in that moment. You do not need to prove your love. You are enforcing space because you care so deeply, not because you do not care. Sometimes it's too much to face head-on. You need a break.

Stay home today. Buy a smoothie. Sit in the sun. The opportunities to touch the memory stones will be there tomorrow. It is okay to enforce space today between you and your grief.

Weighed Down

After a snowstorm, the limbs of the trees are weighed down with snow. The weight of the snow causes them to hang low, just like your head, just like your heart, just like your internal reality after a loss. Being weighed down is not a sin. It is not a bad position, or even a problem. It just is. It is a result of winter. No one likes feeling weighed down, but neither is there a quick fix for it.

Sunlight and warmth are needed to melt the snow on the trees. It's just a matter of time before the sky cracks open with the provision needed to liberate those tree limbs to their intended height. It takes time for something heavy to dissipate.

Time, sunlight, and warmth.
Have grace for yourself.
Winter does not last forever.
And neither will you always be weighed down.

But you, O LORD, are a shield for me; My glory, and the One who lifts my head.

—Psalm 3:3, NKJV

Something to Hold

Sometimes you need something physical to hold that corresponds to your grief. Hopefully, in your days of throwing everything away, you failed to throw everything away and can still find something to hold today.

This may be a paper, a letter, a spoon. It can be anything from a blanket to an unwashed shirt to a seat in the house. Maybe it's a sock you found, a beloved book, or a familiar scent. It could be a place you have not returned to, a restaurant, a park, a car.

Whatever it is, this physical thing will do something for you that cannot be generated through imagination or internal processing. You need something to tell you that this is real. The physical thing validates in a unique way that there is something physically gone. It brings you to a reality that will both sting and heal in the same moment. The healing will last far beyond the sting.

Hold that physical thing even though it might make you feel like a child gripping a teddy bear. You are not regressing in maturity. As you hold it you may also have the thought that you are not a child, this is not a teddy bear, and something must be terribly wrong with you for holding this thing so emotionally tight.

Nothing is wrong. You just need something physical to hold. And that need matters, so hold on. In the holding, let that thing touch you and tell you what you long to hear, which is that the person or thing that is gone is still real.

Sudden Motivation

Suddenly you may find yourself feeling motivated, seemingly out of nowhere. You feel like you could run five miles even though you have not run for months. You remember that things like meal planning and food shopping are a part of life. You become aware that you have not talked with your family in weeks. Unexpectedly, you find that you can see and process more than two inches of your self-parameter.

Embracing this motivation feels difficult. Faster movement feels like a liability. If you speed up and engage in life more, it could lead to a crash. Slow and steady feels safer. You don't understand where this motivation came from or why it is presenting now. Its mysterious entrance leaves you feeling uncertain about its dependability.

What is likely happening is that you just broke through a threshold in your grief. Now grief is not requiring 100 percent of your attention, only 95. That 5 percent is seeing elements of your life that you did not lose with the loss you experienced, things you forgot existed because your grief required all of your focus.

Be encouraged. This motivation is a good indicator that you have put in the hard work to honor your grief to the point where it is relinquishing that 5 percent of your attention to you. Accept it. In it you will discover that your loss has boundaries and there are, believe it or not, still things left in your life for you to do.

The best thing you can do with sudden motivation is milk it for all it is worth. In times like these, you can make progress in days instead of weeks or even months.

Let yourself enjoy the long-lost return of internal motivation. Go get stuff done!

Irritability

Grief makes you feel irritable, like the inside of you is colorless. Anything colorful rubs you the wrong way. Words in general can feel like a personal attack. The internal sense of black and white wants nothing but black and white—nothing. Even if you agree, you cannot bring yourself to agree with anything.

As people talk to you, you find yourself responding in sharp ways. Your heart feels hard, and you don't have the willpower to change it. You can see yourself, as if in the third person, having no room for agreement. You wonder how to limit the potential destructive nature of your attitude without having to change it, which somehow does not feel like a realistic option.

It would be helpful to acknowledge that your irritability is an expression of something real. Your sour attitude is not because of bad motives or a desire to hurt others. It is rooted in your own need to express the unhappiness of your heart. You are unhappy. That is the voice that you and those around you are getting right now. Admitting that you are unhappy can feel like admitting that you are failing in life. It is hard to do. Acceptance, however, can position you for positive change much faster.

In times when happiness is absent, there is a unique invitation to other emotional beauties—internal beauties that irritability (of all things!) can call you straight toward if you let it. There is more to a rich life experience than happiness. A non-performance-demanding presence with yourself is very liberating. Learn how to value your heart and give it a voice, even when it is not sophisticated. Draw away and give yourself permission to stop talking. Discover the power of solitude and silence.

Gratitude can solve irritability very quickly. Find things to be thankful for, one yellow button at a time. The internal power of gratitude is poignant. It does not need to be grandiose, but it does need to be sincere.

Rest assured that irritability will not hold you forever. Something bright will find you eventually and arrest your heart into a forced smile. It is just a matter of time. You are not beyond recovery. You still have the capacity to be cheered up. When cheer comes toward you, go limp toward it and let it hit you with force. In the meantime, don't waste your energy in arguments. The verbal tensions you keep getting trapped in are about your unhappiness. There are always escapes to unhappiness.

It cannot lock its doors. Face the unhappiness. Escape it.

Friendships

Let your friendships change. There are people in your life who have been more loyal to you than your right arm. They watched you succeed and fail while maintaining a commitment that you deeply trust. In your mind, these people are stuck to you like glue. You anticipate that they are the people who will dig in with you now and provide the relational support you so desperately need.

You are finding, however, an odd emotional distance with some of these very people. You know their love for you has not diminished, but their ability to be present with you in your loss seems shallow. Their way of supporting you is giving you "space," which is a novice's response to being with those who grieve.

On the flip side, there are people you hardly know who are showing up for you in ways that feel helpful. They seem to contain that hard-earned ability to stand in the face of emotional pain and therein dare to live with you, not run from you in this epic moment of your story. You fear embracing these people. The thought of making new friends right now is exhausting. You want to cling to your old friends because more change in your life right now is frankly unwelcome.

Let go. Grief will change your friendships. If you resist this, you will be left holding empty clothes with no flesh present. Loss is a destructive blow. Reconstruction after loss is never a replica of what was. It comes with a new design. This can feel terribly unfair because reconstruction from a disaster was not on your bucket list.

It's important to remember that changes in your friendships are most often about people's capacity for grief and about the real changes to your personhood, not about their heart for you. You must accept that those who are unfamiliar with grief do not have much help to give to you right now despite their best intentions. Meanwhile, your shape is changing, and you may become unfamiliar with them, and them with you, rather quickly.

The sooner you accept this, the sooner you will discover that you do not need to be alone in your grief.

You can and will make new friends.

The Trap of Busyness

Sometimes you run to silence and isolation for comfort; other times you grip noise. The latter is actually harder to escape from once you are there.

The tyranny of task will take you by the hands and drag you endlessly forward without permission to sit. Productivity provides momentary rewards, followed by an insatiable need to accomplish more. Busyness can fill space for you, but it will not provide you with the deeper care you need. A dependence on noise will demand more and more noise around you, leaving you with less and less quiet.

Hush.
Hush, child.

The tasks will be there tomorrow.
The demands are less important than they present themselves to be.
The noise cannot hold you well.
There is One who wants to hold you instead.
Dare to cut off the productivity insanity—
And sit.

There is a comfort for you today in the arms of God.

Surely I have stilled and quieted my soul; like a weaned child with his mother, like a weaned child is my soul within me.

—Psalm 131:2, BSB

Be Still

If you are still, you have to face the pain.

If you are still, the reality sets in deeper.

If you are still, memories surface.

If you are still, you discover your restlessness.

If you are still, you may decide to quit.

If you are still …

your heart can breathe.

Your love has wings.

Your grief a voice.

And your soul space.

It is worthwhile to be still. Stillness is where you can touch yourself and determine your own authentic way forward.

Be still.

Be still and know that I am God.

—*Psalm 46:10, BSB*

Part 3: Making Decisions

Aids and Detriments

The following are things that I find either aid or complicate the grief process.

Things that Aid Grief

- Honesty
- Acceptance
- Rawness
- Process
- Time
- Courage

Things that Complicate Grief

- Insensitive People
- Denial
- Pressure
- Expectations
- Isolation
- Silence

You are a powerful person.

Give yourself permission to embrace some things and deny others access to this holy time of your life.

Burial

The process of memorializing a life, the creation of a physical legacy, the consecration of a space for continued remembrance—these are all deeply personal creative endeavors that each person much engage in for him- or herself. There is no right or wrong answer when it comes to whether or not you should do a burial. Every story holds a different path for this, and rightfully so.

That said, I have never met anyone who regretted doing a burial of some kind. I know of many, including myself, who long consider a burial site a sacred gift in the ongoing grief journey. A plot of ground can be purchased in a cemetery, or found on one's property depending on local ordinances. Sit with the concept and you will find your way to a unique expression of your grief in this process.

A burial site creates a place outside of yourself for the loss to sit with dignity. It protects the memory and remains of your loved one for you by holding it underground. This can ease the burden of carrying one's remembrance entirely within yourself. The land becomes sacred—a place that will draw grief out of you when you need it but also hold it quietly for you when you need to be separate from it. It's a space you can walk toward or away from in your grief. A burial site also gives you a physical place to visit and reflect, validating the reality of your loss outside of your own internal life.

If you choose not to do a burial, I validate your decision as well. Some find that legacy gifts honor their loved one more than a grave. Others choose jewelry, tattoos, or a lifetime embrace of a specific color or object. Other people want no physical tokens at all but rather the liberty to outgrow and release the physical aspects of their loss. Some people express honor best through writing or creating associated art or harboring internal and quiet memories. Whatever route you choose, embrace it with confidence.

For those who did not do a burial but want to, it is never too late to bury something in honor of your loved one. You can create that space anytime, in your own time, in your own way.

Your Pace, Your Process

In the immediate days after your loss, you will likely have an ambush of good support. People will feel a lot with and for you. They will come alongside you, give you gifts, offer you meals, and make themselves available to you day and night. In those first few days, your world will stop and see you. You will be cared for.

Then they will move on.

This experience feels like a misfiring of care because in the first few days and weeks of grief, your capacity to receive care is limited by shock and trauma. It is in these initial days after a loss, when your walls are up and your doors are shut, that the entourage of relational support makes its finest performance, only to dwindle when you open your door again and need people the most.

You will watch people go back to their lives within days of your tragedy and return to their joyful existence as if nothing on the earth has changed. You, on the other hand, are left with a world that no longer even looks like planet Earth.

Many people don't understand that tragedies are *day one* of a grief journey that will last the rest of your life. Your life will never be the same. What you suffered was not an event with a start and end time. It was the beginning of a life-long event. It is okay to educate people about this. They are ignorant to what it is like to live with loss.

When people ask you, "What can we do for you?" on day two of your loss, ask them if they would be willing to come back to you with that question in six weeks when you can think more clearly.

When they offer, "How can we help you?" you can ask, "Can you help me celebrate my loved one annually this time of year?"

When they say, "Can we bring you meals?" ask them, "Can

you help me eat well in a few months when I may be facing depression?" Iron out the initial rush of support by encouraging people to come back to you at a future time when you will need them more.

True support for the grieving will exemplify the long-term impact of this loss on your life. It will not dissipate in days, nor will it swallow too deeply whatever you said you needed in those first few days of shock and trauma. Good support will remain present, steady, with you, through the evolving experience and needs of living with loss.

In those moments of feeling left behind, God will never leave you behind. He stays with you. Your pace. Your process. With you.

Throwing Things Away

All of a sudden you feel compelled to throw away all your belongings. You want to donate your clothes, trash your stuff, sell your house. You feel tired of the same old car, the same old windows, the same old silverware. All your stuff seems hopelessly chained to loss triggers. You can't even sit on your furniture without finding the porky pine of grief beneath your bottom. You don't care right now about losing all your belongings, not in light of the one you love being gone. It's hard to perceive a way forward outside of drowning everything you once knew. You consider a decisive castaway of all things that trigger your grief.

There is validity to needing new space, a fresh start, an environment that has a present-future invitation for you rather than a past-present chain. This is something that you will need at some level and move into in time. That said, do not throw everything away at once. Do not throw important things away without pondering them for a few days or weeks. Set things aside, and if you still want to get rid of them in a month or two, then go for it. Sudden decisions to get rid of things may leave you in deeper grief the next morning when you decide that you want that thing back and realize that no replacement will have the memories of what you just chucked.

After you ponder discarding things and you feel ready, let the stuff go. There is a time to release belongings. It is critical to your healing process. If you are visually stimulated, this change of scenery will be particularly necessary for you at some point. That said, there is no rush. You may regret getting rid of things too soon. Take your time.

And don't, please don't throw it all away on the same day. Just because you suddenly can emotionally does not mean you will be glad you did the next morning.

Be Careful with Your Story

Your story is precious. To share your story is to share yourself. In your story, people can discover who you are. In the process of being known, your sense of isolation is broken, giving you a feeling of purpose outside of yourself.

On the other hand, you may be tempted not to share your story because people may not be interested in it. This can feel like a rejection not only of your story but also of you. You find yourself wrestling in almost every interaction. What to share? How much to share? Why share? What will you do if you share and they don't care?

Sometimes you share and it is like dropping a bomb that the person scurries around and away from. Other times you share and it lands gently, with understanding. Often when you share, you get glossy eyes and find yourself interrupted before you are done. Over time you begin to calculate that there is never a time that you share and walk away satisfied with what happened. It is never quite right—always too much, or not enough, or a blaring mistake to have said anything at all.

You are learning that not everyone is safe for your story. Your experience is like a pearl; it is valuable and you cannot trust it in everyone's hands. Some discard it, others want to steal it, some misunderstand it, others couldn't care less. It takes a special person to value rightly what you are carrying right now. You have a pearl.

Protect the most precious parts of your story until you find a safe place to put them. This will spare you perpetual sorrows. Safe people do exist. Wait for them. Default to saying less and wait for the people who ask you for more. The people who want to know you will ask you for more. Others have good intentions, but the depth of what you carry is an anomaly to them, and frankly they do not deserve access to it.

Here's the hard fact: You will always value your story more than the person with whom you are sharing it. This is difficult to swallow, but it is true. You do not need the validation of others to affirm that your story is both deep and heroic. God Himself can do that for you, and with eternal, divine, and kingly sincerity. This divine stamp of approval for your story is a better route to take as the weight of this need on others will set you up for a line-up of disappointing interactions. No one can validate your story like you deserve except for you and God, because no one will ever know your story as deeply as you and God.

Careful with your story.

It is so precious.

Holidays

If you had the opportunity to take a pencil, turn it around, and use it on anything, you would likely apply it to holidays. Holidays feel like a cold bath in your grief. They bring a saturation of triggers and they sting. The trauma of holidays for the grieving is real and so is the dread leading up to them. You feel a forced vulnerability, an unpleasant spotlight on what you are living without. You wish you could skip the holidays, erase them.

Unfortunately, you cannot erase the holidays. They will come. You can choose not to observe them or fly to a distant island that doesn't believe in them. You can decide to pretend that they are not there and busy yourself with other things. But no matter what you do, you cannot erase the holidays. They will come, you will feel their impact, and they will pass.

Fortunately, you can prepare for the holidays—just as you would prepare for a pending storm. Instead of having no plan, make a plan. Instead of pretending it won't happen, prepare for what will happen. Create a place of kindness for yourself in the storm that is coming and it will prove to be a grace for you.

Make your plan. Factor in your honest capacity. This is not a time to commit to being with people with whom you already had a hard time before your grief. This is not a time to assume that you will be "just fine" doing all the normal holiday things. This is a time to think about what could make the holiday special for you as a grieving person. It is a time to think about "kindness to self" and try to ace that game.

Prepare a space in the holiday for you to celebrate and honor the one you miss. Even the smallest tribute, prepared ahead of time, will give you space to breathe on that day.

Make a plan, and be encouraged that it will all be over soon.

Thankfully for the grieving, the holidays do end.

To Those Who Grieve on Christmas

It can be easy to feel like you are crawling along on the outskirts of Christmas, pressed outside the worldwide joy parade by a sorrowful circumstance. You are watching the holiday happen, trying hard not to be sad while the world sings "Glory!" The festivities feel more like arrows to your heart than gifts, the sounds and visuals of the holiday a blaring reminder of what you are living without. In particular, if it is your first Christmas without a loved one, it is likely no less than a hike up Mount Everest to make it through this season emotionally. Christmas holds amplified emptiness when those we love are not with us in it.

I have a word for you. Hear me, beloved! You are not on the outskirts of Christmas. Do you know what everyone is gathered around? They are celebrating the coming of King Jesus, who is a man familiar with sorrow and well-acquainted with grief. I believe that every single twinkling light is a sign that there is hope for those who are brokenhearted. Jesus came and courageously pursued those who were most hurting. He is still doing this very thing today, on Christmas. His eyes and heart are toward you. You are not alone. You are not outside of what Christmas is about. You are actually the reason for this season.

You are the reason He came.

You grumpy, grieving, sorrowful, and beautiful person.

Perhaps feeling very much alone.

> *The LORD is near to the brokenhearted And saves those who are crushed in spirit.*
>
> —*Psalm 34:18, NASB*

Christmas is a holiday about Jesus, and Jesus sees you in your grief and loves you more deeply than anyone ever could. He is near to you, nearer than your breath. It is possible to be comforted on Christmas day and benefit deeply from the good news that sits at the core of this holiday. Jesus came, and is still coming, to save, rescue, and redeem those who are hurting. I declare to you, beauty for ashes, joy for mourning, and praise for despair. Isaiah 61:1-3 belongs to you! Unwrap it. It's all yours. You are at the center of what this day is about.

My love to the grieving on Christmas.

Christ's love to the grieving on Christmas.

Be seen. Be loved.

This day is about *you*, the coming of your Savior.

Using Names

Names hold identities. There is no reason why you need to stop using your loved one's name. It makes some people uncomfortable, but so do many other things that we would never wrap our behaviors around in good conscience.

Do you miss hearing their name? Do you want to use their name? Do you want to engrave it somewhere? Do you want to find a space for their name to live on? Then do it.

"I miss Ruby today" is more direct than "I miss my daughter today." It preserves a unique identity that I want living on with me. I use my daughter's name a lot. People who never met her know her name.

I encourage you to remove that odd mouth guard that is offered to the grieving when it comes to using someone's name who passed away. Let that name roll off your tongue when it wants to. Determine that when it comes to your brain, it will also find its way out of your mouth. Preserve names, not as a chore but as a gift.

Protecting Your Beliefs

In times of disappointment there is the temptation to start throwing in the towel on convictions that you long held dear. Inside you feel more like a victim than an overcomer. This causes you to identify as someone who is losing everything without a choice in the matter. You lack conviction that there is power or value in holding on to your worldview and beliefs. The situation you are in feels so far outside of your control that you could let your beliefs run away in a dance with its swirling uncertainties.

The perception that you are a victim could not be further from reality and must be confronted. You are an overcomer. Victims do not have choices; you still have choices. Perhaps they are not the choices that you want, but you do have them. If nothing else, you can choose which way you are running with your pain, where you are taking it, if it is leading you into depression or you are leading it into the arms of God. You can choose the convictions that you want to herald, the beliefs you will protect, the worldview you will hold. For me, I could not choose to heal my daughter and bring her back to life, but I could choose not to give up on my belief that God heals today. This decision to grip my convictions in the face of a mystery forged a trajectory of opportunity in my life that would otherwise have sunk in grief.

You have a loss, a disappointment, a space of mystery in your life. That space is sacred, and it matters. That space, however, is not all space. Loss, disappointment, and mystery do not need to take over your identity. You have beliefs that preceded this loss and will exist far beyond it. Protect those beliefs. If you are careful to protect your convictions, even in the face of disappointment, your convictions will end up defining your loss rather than your loss defining your convictions.

Be careful what you are willing to lose right now.
Hang on tightly to your convictions.
Truth does not always subject itself to our experience,
But it will forge your experience into beauty if you hold on to it.
Don't give up on your beliefs.

Part 4: Staying Healthy

Getting Your Needs Met

You are accustomed to getting your needs met in a certain way, and in your grief you are stubbornly looking for that same provision and finding it gone. The place where your needs were met is no longer there. This does not mean you have to live with dangling unmet needs. It does mean that it is time to trail blaze new ways to get your needs met. Your sense of justice will resist learning new routes for meeting needs because it is not fair. It is, however, liberating, strengthening, and maturing.

There is a profound opportunity here to grow a more authentic expression of yourself. You so identified yourself with another person, place, or thing that in the rewiring of your needs you will enter into a self-discovery process that will yield deep satisfaction in time. You get to redefine your needs and pave the road to healthy sources of support. This can be exciting if you see it as a beautiful and long-awaited life renovation.

Honor your needs. Take time to define them. Let them lead you to new soil. Listen to yourself. Get acquainted with yourself. Dare to know yourself. Dare to bring your known self to God.

An intentional collision with God can solve the unmet-need category very quickly. He knows you. He knows your history. He knows your present. He knows your future. He is your future. God knows how your needs were met and He knows how to meet your needs now. He is not second best at it. He is first. He is constant. God is here to help you pave new roads to get your needs met.

Personal Hygiene

After my daughter Ruby passed away, I did not want to shower. I did not want to bathe. I did not want the laundry done. I wanted nothing to be cleaned that she had touched, not even myself. The thought of putting things in the washing machine felt like ringing out the reality that she was gone. Washing myself felt like washing away my proximity to her. As long as there were things she had physically touched, we could not be that far apart. That is how I felt.

There is something about cleanliness that separates what was from what is. When you step out of the shower, it is somehow a new start. For those who grieve, the newer the start, the further away your loved one feels. Holding on to things in their present condition feels like holding time hostage.

The ability to clean up, clean yourself, and clean out will come. It may never force itself on you. You will likely at some point need to stand up and choose it. But the grace to do it will come. When that happens, rest assured that there is a beautiful transition that awaits you in it.

Your attempts to freeze time are actually causing you greater distance from where your loved one now lives, fully alive. He or she beat you home. When you clean up, you will feel more connected to the reality that now holds your loved one's new life in eternity and your ongoing life here. Cleanliness will somehow liberate you from the sterile space they left behind and release you into the wonder of where they have gone and where you now are.

Anger

You are generally not an angry person. That word would be one of the last to describe your personality. However, in these days you find yourself easily angered. Your capacity for people's nonsense is very shallow, and your tendency to blame others for your pain incredibly free flowing.

Anger is not soft, accommodating, or safe. It is also not wrong. Anger is a valid protector for a hurting heart. It valiantly takes the front burner of your soul and there makes sure that the heart is kept safe. Safety for your heart is important because it is hurting. It makes sense that you feel angry.

Anger is almost always an expression of pain. It is the sound of pain coming out of the heart. It will protect your pain and destroy your relationships. Anger has an unruly ability to destroy whatever gets close to it. It can turn the closest friends into enemies quickly. You must learn to move through it and not get stuck in it, which takes humility. Quick repentance will preserve a lot in your life in this season.

In order to process anger well, you must recognize that it is seldom an enemy. Most often, anger is playing an important role for you. It is a validator of emotional pain. It is an expression of your soul with a noble goal. It is part of the healing process. Anger is not a page to blot out but rather a segment of a trail to conquer. You must take care to conquer it so that it does not conquer you.

Two questions that will help you process anger with emotional health include:

"What hurt is beneath this anger?" and

"What is this anger protecting me from?"

In these reflections, you will find that anger is a profound narrator of things that matter to your heart.

Anger reveals things you were long disturbed by but failed to acknowledge.

Anger amplifies impacts you harbored inside without a voice.

Anger is present to do something about injustices that are lying dormant in your life.

Anger brings forward the sound of pain so that it is heard as an important emotional experience in grief.

Anger is designed to be a signal, not a way of life. Let the signal lead you to the deeper truths about your heart, your voice, and your needs. Don't get stuck with the alarm going off on repeat. Let it wake you up and lead you onward. Only in dealing with the undercurrents of the anger will you find the healing your heart so needs. No need to lose your personality in grief, beloved. Some do, but you do not need to. Take care not to become an angry person on repeat.

Sleep

Sometimes all you want to do is sleep. It feels like a harmless escape. It doesn't solve the pain, but it does provide a muted experience of it, for a few hours.

When you wake up there are two seconds when you don't fully remember the pain you are living with. In those two seconds, you take your only two breaths of the day. The rest of the time you are holding your breath in some measure so as not to yield yourself to the impact of what you are enduring in your heart. You hold your breath, waiting until you can sleep again.

What if you wake up? What if you never wake up again? Which is worse? Which is better? Which is more conducive to life?

If you utilize sleep as an escape, you will also begin to fear it, and rightfully so as it could swallow you whole. The remedy to this fear is not to force yourself to stay awake but to recognize that sleep is a kindness when both sides of its offering are fully accepted.

Sometimes the kindest thing you can do for yourself is give yourself permission to sleep. Other times the kindest thing you can do for yourself is force yourself to get back up. You must discern for yourself what time calls for which. Be honest about what seems healthy to you in the moment and choose the healthy thing, for your own sake. You must learn to see both the lying down *and* the getting back up as their own unique hug for you as you grieve.

Sleep is not an enemy; it is a kindness—a kindness that is only kind when both parts of its equation are active.

Lie down.

Get up again.

Get up again.

Physical Symptoms

You were accustomed to good health in your life, but now that you are grieving, pains seem to emerge out of nowhere. Rashes appear. Headaches present. Digestion changes. Vision seems impaired. You experience muscular weakness, lightheadedness, tooth pain, back pain, and a compromised immune system. Other random physical symptoms appear without explanation. The symptoms come and go, one at a time. Sometimes they overlap with one another. You wonder if you are terminally ill. That seems the most probable explanation in the context of your grief.

You go to the doctor. They cannot find anything wrong. Despite your internal fatal narrative, medical tests are done and they all come back normal. Shocking. You expected bad news but got none. They tell you that you are healthy. "Healthy" doesn't seem like a rational explanation for your pain. You begin to wonder if it's possible that all these mysterious new physical symptoms are rooted in your grief. They are.

Your body is manifesting emotional pain. Excess grief is escaping through your body because there is not enough room for it in the soul. The weight of your sadness is spilling out. Medical treatments alone are unlikely to succeed in solving these issues. You need to broaden your release valve for grief.

Grief must be addressed at the soul level, and primary in that realm is finding expression for what you are feeling emotionally. Buy a journal. Write. Draw, even if you never have. Scribble, paint, break a glass. Document a piece of your story: visit the cemetery. Take a day off from work: drive somewhere you feel safe and scream, cry. Find someone who will listen. Express your grief. This will divert its path from your physical body.

When it comes to the pain of grief, you have the choice of focusing solely on the physical ailment or exerting the discipline to also address the deeper needs of your soul. The former will likely lead you down a trail of medications that does not easily end. The latter will be a rewarding course in discerning the voice of your heart and responding to it. Consider treating your soul and not just your body. A holistic approach to care will likely yield better relief. Regardless of what you choose, be encouraged that your body will be fine. You are not terminally ill. Your energy will return. Your days of pain-free existence are not over. You will feel good again.

Your body is sounding an alarm.

Your job is to listen to it.

Get the emotional release valve open.

Give your grief space.

It will prove a healing grace.

Your heart deserves to be heard.

Seeing Past Yourself

There are people around you who still need you. Yet this feels unfair to you. The noise inside of you is so intense that any noise outside of you is too much noise, even if it is coming from those you love. You are drained. Demands on you feel cruel. You think that what you need most is to be all alone in bed with the covers over your head. *I should not have to be anything for other people right now.*

From your own state of blindness, you determine that no one else exists right now as far as you are concerned. You feel no motivation to help others. Not now. The problem with this rationale is that it assumes that people are your enemy right now, and some are not. The people who need you are not monsters in search of blood. They are specific human beings who validate your importance on the earth through their need of you. People who need you are the infrastructure of purpose that you still have left.

Purpose is always found outside yourself. It is never a solo experience. If you can see past yourself for a moment and serve the people in need of you, you will simultaneously release yourself from a space drained of purpose.

I dare you to see people's needs as validation of your importance and not as a threat to your grief. If you can see past yourself and care for them, in that act you will unwrap the purpose that still sits in your life right now.

This is a very important discovery, for them but also for you.

Negativity

There is a difference between honest expression and freelance negativity. The former is grace-filled and necessary. The latter is harmful and threatening. You deserve a safe place to be honest, fully honest. You need permission to be honest both with yourself and with others. If you do not have this, you will feel restricted in life and stuck in your grief process. The sense of internal heaviness will grow very strong until you feel deeply hidden behind the façade that people see. Your communication will become shallow—nothing more than a space-filler in the face of your silent need to share yourself.

It is critical that you have a place to honestly express yourself. If you do not, this legitimate need will find other outlets in your life, perhaps unhealthy, and perhaps without your permission. That said, if negativity is the overall flavor of your expression, it will intoxicate your heart very quickly. Negativity sees one side of things —the bad side. It does not have language for the good in people, places, or things. It is thoroughly convinced of itself and very narrow-minded in its approach. It requires no authentication, except for an internal mental agreement. It can destroy purity quickly, like a drop of red ink in water. The drop seems harmless, but the effect is toxic.

Observe the overall tone of your expression. If it is all negative, spare yourself being poisoned slowly by your own words and put that ink away. There is a better way of meeting your need for honesty, one that can honestly acknowledge that there is more than one thing happening.

Both positive and negative experiences are part of your life right now, and both need a voice in your expression. Both are present. Both are real. Both phone lines open will provide you with a choice that you desperately need. If you hang up the phone on positivity, you are cutting yourself off from half your options on a way forward.

Dare I point out the brighter half?

Comfort Food

You are consuming more and more food. As you eat, you feel somewhat detached from yourself, as if a part of you is starving without consolation. You are observing yourself, as if in the third person, eating with increased carelessness.

There is something emotionally soothing about being physically full. When you are physically full, you feel less emotionally empty. That experience keeps you reaching for food. The problem is that meeting emotional needs with food is a recipe for greater illness. It will end up making you sick and disgusted with yourself. Food will never be enough to solve the needs of your broken heart.

The apathy you feel about your diet has now opened a door to shame. You find yourself eating more, alone, embarrassed of what people will think if they see you eat. You begin to hide your true eating habits, at which point they plummet. Before you know it, food becomes a god that you serve instead of it serving you. If you do not protect yourself from this, you will implode in your grief.

You deserve better care than what food has to offer you.

My advice is to fast for a day or two. Cut off this food dependency and find your way back home to dependency on God. The Holy Spirit can provide you with the comfort you need. There is no comfort that compares to what He has to offer you, and it will not cost you your personal dignity.

Get help if you need it. Pull that starving part of yourself back into your core self. Lead it with dignity to Jesus instead of letting it lead you with shame to addiction.

Building Walls

You are finding that the closest people to you, while well-intentioned, are insensitive to your needs. Grief is a foreign language to them and they are misfiring in their "care" for you. You try to be gracious and explain what you need. They look back at you like you have ten heads and then do or say the same thing again, seemingly deaf to what you expressed.

> You're tired of trying to explain yourself.
> You're tired of being your own advocate.
> You're tired of hoping to be loved in a way you can feel it, and instead find salt on your wound.

> So… you build walls.
> Farewell, presence.
> Hello, withdrawal.

What you don't see clearly as your walls go up is that your decision to withdraw is a form of firing back on someone you love. And likely misfiring. Their intention is not to hurt you. You have a hard time believing that because their insensitivity seems like a straightforward violation of common sense. You feel that they should understand the intricate care of a heart injury without an education. It's life; it's common sense. Friendship 101.

Is it common sense to someone who has never known the injury from which you suffer? Maybe not.

> Maybe your friend needs an education.
> And if they do, are you willing to give it?
> To protect the relationship?

Walls do not come down as easily as they go up.
Take care when choosing them.
Perhaps don't build them so quickly.
The work of deconstruction takes effort.

Serving Others

Your motivation is crawling. Making yourself dinner takes a lot of energy, let alone getting out of the house to engage in something outside your mandatory routine. When you are out, you look forward to being home where you are not under observation. You keep your home rather dark and have not had anyone in it for some time.

An opportunity arises to serve someone else. You consider whether you have the capacity for this. You calculate that you do not.

Advice: do it anyway. Go!

Serve others.

Don't stop serving others.

Serving is a drawbridge out of the outdated fortress you silently ache to leave. There is liberty in being forced to see beyond yourself and into the life of another person. When a flow of care moves through you and lands on another, it will provide a new flow of life through your own system. Joy can be found through serving, even in the darkest season. Serve others.

The Need for Nature

I heard of a man who was diagnosed with a terminal disease. His response was to move to the beach. He pitched a tent by the water and spent as much time in the ocean breeze as possible, with a firm commitment to natural foods. For months he absorbed the care of nature. A year later he had a clean bill of health.

If this were a guaranteed remedy for all disease, the terminally ill would all be cured by now, beachfront resorts replacing hospitals with windows wide open to real air. Or would they? Do we believe in this? Do we prioritize it?

Natural healing remedies are largely ignored in our culture. We lock the sick up in rooms with no open windows, in spaces without sunlight, in corners far from bodies of water. We give them white walls to stare at instead of trees or artwork. Beeping monitors and white noise underscore the space instead of engaging with the power of music.

As one who grieves, I recommend natural beauty as part of your prescribed care. It holds healing for you that will penetrate to your deepest self without a single side effect. Its gentle graces can enable you to breathe again, see again, hope again, and dream again. Nature is a God-designed space, full of power and grace. God can use nature to meet you in the lowliest of sorrows and show you the trail from there to the heights of peace.

If you live in a basement, move out. If you live in a perpetual winter, escape for a weekend. If you have not seen the sun in a while, chase it until it is strong enough to tinge your skin. If your eyes have not beheld a mountain a thousand times your size, please go find one. If you have not sat in the ocean breeze for more than an hour in the last year, you must go.

Nature's beauty holds a mystery of healing that will deeply grace your journey if you will carve out the time for it. It is one of those things that will not come to you; you must go to it. That in itself is part of the healing experience.

Celebrate Each Step

The man looked me square in the eyes with an intensity of courage that only emerges through the bedrock of one's own suffering. He had lost his wife years ago to a disease. My husband and I sat before him as bereaved parents looking for help. Our daughter was nearly three years old when she burst through the confines of this world and beat us Home. We were left alone. This man was a pastor; he was alone too. Maybe he could help us find our way out of this dark maze of what life had become.

"Sometimes survival is a noble goal," he said.

To many that statement would seem bleak at best. To me, however, it was the first encouraging thing I had heard in a long time. Why? It honored me. His statement hosted an understanding that what I needed most was to celebrate the triumph of each step. Maybe I was still having a hard time getting out of bed. Maybe I was still crying a lot. Maybe I was not fun to be with, and my sense of purpose was a lost puppy at best. But maybe arising each day took courage, and living itself was a noble goal.

Sometimes all people need to heal is honor. People need to know that they have strength before they will exert the strength to heal. You and I get to tell others about their strength through authentic and heart-felt honor. Honor excavates courage in people, and in so doing it liberates their capacity to hold their own redemption from Jesus.

Today, I honor you. I honor you for not giving up inside of the intensity of your story. I thank you for choosing not to let your heart grow cold or numb in the face of such pain. Thank you for continuing to love God and serve others despite all the opposition. Thank you for not giving up, friends. Thank you for embracing the noble goal of continuing, one day at a time.

Be encouraged.
Your Father sees.
And celebrates.
You.

He honors you *today*.
And so do I.

Be crowned.
Be honored.
You deserve it.
Oh, strong one!
Celebrate each step.

Part 5: Exerting Courage

Moving Forward

What you love is in your past. You want to move forward but every step forward feels like a betrayal to what is behind you. Proximity to the past feels like loyalty to what you love. Moving forward feels like a betrayal to the one you love.

You feel safest emotionally in refusing to move forward. Standing close to your loss, you will be the first to know when it changes its mind and repents from reality. You remain in earshot so that its call of repentance is not lost by your distance. You stand ready to pick up where you left off and re-engage the love you knew.

What are the odds that this is going to change?

How much will you lose waiting for it to change?

How much can you gain by moving forward?

Listen to me. What you love is ahead of you. It is not behind you. Every step forward you take is one step closer to rediscovering what you love. The loss is behind you; the gain is ahead of you. The tragedy is behind you; the rebirth of your soul is ahead of you. The separation is behind you; the reunion is ahead of you.

The last time you saw what you loved, it was in the past. You think it is still there because that is the last time that you saw it. It is no longer there. I am telling you, it is no longer there. If it was a person, he or she beat you Home and is now standing far ahead of you in your future.

Your past is empty of opportunities and offers no promise to regenerate new outcomes. Your past can only birth a new beauty when it connects with your future. You do not need to remain in proximity to your tragedy to honor it. The thing that you love is no longer there. Honoring the one you love looks like exerting the courage to love yourself by getting unstuck

and embracing the life that you still have left to live.
What you love is ahead of you.
Dare to move forward.

Coming Out of Hiding

Grief gave you a reason to hide. While hiddenness expands the isolation in your life, it also gives you a shield. This shield is valiant, stamped with the seal of someone who has suffered a real loss and is overcoming with courage privately. It's a shield that not everyone has the strength to wield, but it is in your hands, and people respect it. They will leave you alone when you get behind it.

Brilliant as you are, you have found that this shield can be used for more than just grief. It proves a gift in erasing the need for excuses to not engage in certain things or with certain people whom you have honestly not liked, even long before you were grieving. You can now excuse yourself from the need to find a valid excuse for absence and simply use your shield to not engage in things you have long despised.

In time, you find that the shield does not have a set boundary; it can grow. It has the ability to become a pillar, a column, even a wall, or in time a fortress. The less you come out from behind it, the more it expands its reach, and the harder it becomes to consider living without it. *Ta-da!* A safe life. A life alone.

Hear me. Life behind a shield is not one you want to find yourself trapped in. It is time to exert courage to show up again in a few things that you have not missed. I repeat, these are things you have not missed. Grief has given you a distance from certain things and that was a kindness to you. You can either show up again to these things or accept that these things will have drowned in neglect. There is no right or wrong choice here, but from one friend to another I do think it is important that your choice be informed.

The things you are hiding from are growing very distant from you.

You may want to consider coming out soon.

That Same Old Feeling

You woke up today and found yourself in a place of sorrow that you worked hard to navigate away from countless times. It's that same old feeling: grief encompassing everything; fogginess settling in like a tyrant over your day. You did not feel this bad yesterday. You wonder what caused the regression.

You sit up to face your day, wrapped in the question of whether you have made any progress in grief at all, and whether the work of forward motion is worthwhile since you seem to be catapulted back without warning or reason. I get it. I know. It's discouraging.

The bright spot here, that you may fail to see in the moment, is that the intervals of consuming grief are widening. Healing is not measured by decreasing sadness but by increasing time between the sadness that debilitates you. You still have a reason to be sad. The loss is still there. In fact, today is a brand-new experience of it.

The important thing today is to give yourself permission to be where you are and continue forward from there. No need to be discouraged. You are surely progressing in your grief. Your need for noted progress can be settled in discovering that these days are becoming less frequent; the intervals are widening.

Let this wave of grief bring you remembrances of your love. You can cherish what you feel as a recall to the love in your heart. You grieve because you love. This "same old feeling" is not a measurement of your progress; it's a remembrance of your love.

Embracing Change

Grief is changing you. This change can be healthy, a liberating process. Your grief is like a crucible that is exposing the real nature of things in your life. It is burning away the façade and exposing what is really there. As you embrace change within yourself, your relationships will also change. You will outgrow them. You will outgrow a lot.

There is much more for you in life: more beauty, more connections, more success, more advancement, more wonder, more adventure, and more space for you to be who you really are. Don't deny the changes in your life and friendships. The depth of who you are becoming is remarkable. Your heart is outgrowing its old space in a brilliant way. You are changing, and so is your life. Denial of this will not stop the change, but it will keep you from its benefits.

You may feel inclined to resist outgrowing your old space. Let go. You can do this. Embrace change. You will be thankful in time that you are no longer restricted to the life you once had or the person you were.

The grief process contains layers of new adjustments, each a brilliant invitation into a more authentic self. Keep advancing. Let change happen. This is not a hamster wheel; it's a metamorphosis. Don't quit!

Social Settings

You went to a party, a baby shower, a holiday gathering, a wedding, a birthday celebration, a dinner. There you found yourself in mild shock. Everyone seemed half drunk on a life that is a distant memory to you. They were happy, merry, and seemed acquainted with bliss. To you they all seem trapped in a bubble, a bubble you lost track of a long time ago.

No one noted the courage it took for you to show up. Being surrounded by people is a mountain to climb for you right now, let alone a gathering of happy people who are as unfamiliar with suffering as a bird is to the deep sea.

You spend half the time, at least, planning your exit strategy. On the way home, you consider giving up on social settings altogether. They drain your energy and leave you worse off than when you came. It seems like a better idea to stay hidden in your grief where happy people cannot poke your pain so easily.

All I really want to say to you is, "Good job for showing up!" That courage will carry you far. It is the very thing that will pull you up out of darkness in time. You may have hated the experience, but at least you went!

The more you show up, the more you will find your place in these gatherings. Your place will be different than it once was. You will likely begin to find others who are feeling much like you are, and you will become a tent of safety in the needles of social life, providing the opportunity for deep connection where it is craved. In the meantime, reward yourself for going. Really. Celebrate yourself every time you go.

A grieving person stepping into a social setting is like a bungee jumper taking the leap. It's a terrible free fall the entire time until a sudden catch of a rope leaves you hanging in midair, perhaps upside down. The rope eventually carries you back up to land, not nearly fast enough, while you hang at its mercy with nothing more to show for the intensity of your experience than whiplash—and, oh, a paper certificate for taking the leap. Don't skip the certificate. I am handing it to you now: "Courageous Isolation Breaker."

Good job.

Facing Another Day

You woke up sad again. The first few waking moments held hot pain that makes you dread the day. If you could sit alone all day and stare out the window, you would and could. And yet, you can't. Life is rolling onward. Somehow you have to find a way to show up to another day. If you can just get through this day, you only have one more day to go before you need to get through another day.

Consider that this day has never presented before. Things will transpire for the very first time today, things that could bring a sense of relief and joy to you. No day is entirely predictable. Perhaps this one is holding a few buds of promise in your favor. You won't know until you step into it, eyes open. Don't be afraid to engage with your day; it may be holding what your heart needs. Maybe it will be wonderful and surprising. I hope—with and for you—that today will prove to be that and more.

Reentry

Reentry into "normal life" after a loss can be jolting. You step in and hold your breath; you step out and unravel. You step in and hold your tongue; you step out and vent. You step in and take steps forward; you step out and quit. You step in; you step out. You brace yourself; you crash. You live a dichotomous life that no one understands. Your internal reality is worlds away from the external world that demands your presence daily.

In the bumpy transitions between your inward and outward journey, it can help to find low-threshold social settings for soft practice. These are settings that do not require you to do much, say much, or be much of anything apart from physically present. For example, when you are watching a movie with someone, you don't have to talk. When you are at a performance, you don't have to produce. When you are sitting in a class, you don't have to come up with the curriculum.

Find settings where others hold the responsibility for what takes place and you can be a passive participant. These settings will help you acclimate to being with people without the added pressure to produce and perform. Start with low-threshold settings. Build up from there. Slowly.

Reasons to Continue

Sometimes it is hard to put one foot in front of another. Moving forward feels like treading through mud. You wonder if it's worth it. You wonder why you are doing it. You look for one good reason to continue living.

> One good reason to continue living.
> Can you think of one?
> Can you think of two?
> Can you think of ten?

No one lasts in a mud trek for long without a reason to continue on. Give this some thought; it will loosen the mud from your shoes faster. Concrete motivation will move you through all this faster. It will liberate you from the drudgery faster.

> *Because I might have my own baby someday.*
> *Because I love Mitch and want to see him reach his destiny.*
> *Because the ocean is here.*
> *Because the sun still wants to kiss me.*
> *Because I have more to write.*

Seasons Will Change

Your loss seemingly has no end in sight. Seeking closure feels like chasing vapor. The "find the new normal" concept is not helping. You feel thrust into a new state of being that is plagued with a crisis that may never die.

While this has validity, it is important to also see that the tragedy itself, the event, is in the past. The winter, as it were, is over. The impact is devastating and still with you, but even so the winter itself is past. Winter does not last forever. You may not care if winter is over or not at this point in your journey, since there is no guarantee you will not face another winter in time. The avoidance of tragedy in life is no more productive than trying to de-pickle a cucumber. We are saturated in a human experience that holds very few guarantees. And yet you will find that if you do face another tragedy, it will not impact you like the one that you just went through. You gained a lot of strength through this experience, and it is quite possible that the worst days of your life are behind you. Consider *that*.

The winter is past. This is important for you to know because you will not plant anything, take your coat off, or adventure outdoors during the winter. There are a slew of things that you simply will not do until you know that the winter is over. Somehow, somewhere, in all this waterfall of tragedy, there is something that is over. I dare you to find it and let it lead you to the first buds of spring.

You may have just conquered the darkest days of your life.

The winter is past.

At least something of that winter is over.

What is it? What is over and done?

For now the winter is past; the rain is over and gone. The flowers have appeared in the countryside; the season of singing has come, and the cooing of turtledoves is heard in our land.

—Song of Solomon 2:11-12, BSB

Courage to Trust Again

You have come a long way in your grief. Many of the shadows that used to hold you back are no longer with you. The landscape of your life has changed. People you meet now don't know your story. You don't feel the same need you once did to disclose it all, again and again. Your own ground zero has progressed into something that could produce new growth—and already is on some level.

The problem is that you do not trust anyone. It is impossible to rebuild a meaningful life without some level of trust. The experience of having something so precious ripped away from you left you with an unwelcome awareness that it can happen again. You conclude that you will be less susceptible to another loss if you keep your heart away from people who require trust.

In time you realize, however, that this is no way to live. When the heart is bound, life is a burden. You decide to take a risk. You connect with someone or something at the heart level. In it you begin to awaken from your grief in a brand-new way. You discover that there are large aspects of recovery that were held on the other side of a new heart connection in your life. Trust brings a depth of healing that is reserved for the brave.

If the first heart connection you make out of grief grows into a healthy tree, you will find yourself invited out of the disaster zone of your life and into a brand-new home. If a disappointment occurs, you will be tempted to take it as a fatal emotional crash with a long pause before you attempt it again.

I believe you can be safe in learning to trust again regardless of the outcome of the first connection. The first connection is fragile, regardless of whether it is a person, place, or thing. Your focus needs to remain on your progress in daring to trust again, not on the outcome of that first connection. Mark every step of progress you make in daring to trust again and keep your own forward momentum in focus. Whether this first connection thrives or not, your effort in it demonstrates the tackling of something that no one but you can take away from you.

It is worth trusting again, risking again, loving again. Your life is not over. Don't quit on it prematurely. Step forward. Take hold of something new. You can do it.

Part 6: Pacing Your Process

Permission to Be Happy

There is little as frightening as happiness when you are grieving. It comes with a brief sense of bliss, like being handed a bright-red helium balloon. You stare at it in wonder and consider if it is worth the work of adopting it. You wonder where it belongs. There is no good place to put it, no cupboard space designed for a balloon, no shelf cut out for its round air-filled waiting-to-pop self. It seems to belong nowhere, except in your hands, for a few minutes while it lasts.

Happiness is scary because it is momentary. You wish to be happy all the time. If you embrace happiness for five minutes, one evening, or a single weekend, then you have to experience deflation again whenever that happiness pops and falls to the ground as shriveled rubber. The balloon deflates, the sun sets, the ice cream bowl is empty, your company leaves, your new shoes get scuffed, and that happy moment dissipates. It ends. *But who's to say that you will not be better off from its visit?*

The grieving often stare at happiness with the most severe distrust, almost always at a distance until it deflates. They refuse to touch it, let alone take hold of it. My questions to you are these:

What if happiness has value even if it is fleeting?
What if the best of happiness is delivered inside of what is otherwise not a happy time?
What if you and I need happiness like we need air?
What if it is worth being happy for one hour even if you are sad again later?

Weigh it. I believe that you will find that happiness is worth it.

Happiness by nature is fleeting. That is part of its beauty. It shimmers with fragility, rarity, and finds its value in the way it stands apart. It lives best in framed moments. If you receive the balloon, you may also have to lose the balloon. And yet those who have once held a balloon are generally happier than those who have never held one.

You have permission to be happy. Take the balloon. It will remind your heart that life can be good. It's like sunlight; you need it to survive. You have permission to be happy. Take the balloon. Just take it.

Catapulted Backward

A touchstone of familiarity from the past found its way to you. Suddenly you are spinning as if the change in your life just happened. Your loss feels so close that it appears it could reverse itself. You find yourself holding your breath in hopes of just that. The progress you made moving forward dissipates so fast you wonder if it was a vapor to begin with. *What is the point*, you ask yourself, *of all this hard-earned forward movement if it can be swallowed up so suddenly by something seemingly so small?*

Catapulted backward, you are now faced with an internal longing for the past that is digging its heals into your mental process. You remember your life before loss. Touching that familiarity gives you great relief and great pain in the same moment. Emotional proximity reacquaints you with the self you once knew, which highlights how confused you are about who you are now. You can remember when every day was not plagued by the work of sorting out reality. You want that life back. You can taste it.

The familiar will always expose what love is left in you for that person, place, or thing. It can pierce the layers of "progress" and fiercely tear them down in a moment. It can also expose that your heart is still alive. And that is a testament to your strength. Your heart is surviving despite the crushing blow of your experience. You still feel because you still care. You are likely still waiting for justice.

The exposure of your pain is an opportunity to heal in a deeper way. If you stand back up after a catapult backward, then you will find an inner strength forming that is unassailable. It is no small thing to rise again, and again. Nothing can keep you from moving forward except for yourself, not even a catapult backward.

Gentleness

You need gentleness. Small pressures hurt badly. Your capacity feels limited, like the limited capacity of a bruise to push back on pressure.

Inside of your heart there is a deep longing to be well. Lately you have been pushing yourself rather hard to that end. This is a reminder that you suffered a hard impact not too long ago. Be gentle with yourself.

Making Ongoing Memories

It is good to continue making memories that are for and about your loved one, even after they are gone. Why? They are not really gone. They are alive. They are more alive than you are. We are the ones who are still dying.

Maybe it's a certain dessert, a song, a spot at the beach, a pet, a pen, or a space in the house. Perhaps it's a date on the calendar, or a holiday embraced, a trip, a location, an object you purchase, an experience. You can find things to do in honor of your loved one that connects you to their life, past and present.

I am not talking about "visiting the dying." I am talking about living aware of the living. Permission granted. There is more to life than this side of eternity. The other side is where your loved one now lives. Beyond that veil. Key word: lives.

Do you really think there are no birthdays there?

Giving Up

You can give up.
Sometimes you need to.

But how about *you* decide what you are giving up on and for how long. How about you take ownership of that decision instead of letting your circumstances dictate it for you. If you are going to give up, do it on purpose, not as a victim. This way your surrender will land in your benefit and not to your detriment.

The white flag will find its way into your hands.
You will wave it at some point.

When you find it in your hands, my advice is to use it to protect yourself, not as a signal that you are disarming what you value. Give up to stay safe, not to lose more on top of your loss. Take care what you are willing to lose in this time.

Surrender forward, not backward.
Surrender as royalty does: to gain and not lose.

Short-term Memories

Grief requires a lot of mental energy. Your brain activity is intensely focused right now on persevering through each day. Long-term memories are pressed by grief into back rooms where they seemingly cease to exist. You may find that your short-term memory is also muted, dull at best, and fear that it may not return.

This is normal, and it is not permanent.

Rest assured, your memory will return.

In time, you will find yourself recalling things about your life, history, interests, aspirations, and dreams outside of this present loss. It will surprise you, but you will in time greet old memories that float back to the front of your consciousness. As grief is honored and worked through, it will relent its hold on your memories. Your way of remembering will return to normal.

I recall saying to a minister, "It all died with her. My dreams died, my aspirations died, my hopes died, my sense of purpose died. I have no idea who I am now."

He answered me, "Did you die?"

"No."

"Well, then neither did your dreams. If you are still here, they are still here inside of you, although presently quiet. They will re-emerge after grief loosens its grip."

And they did.

Two Steps Forward, One Step Back

Two steps forward.
One step back.

The step back feels unbearable emotionally. You now want to quit. You feel like you will never get better; sorrow seems like your sentence in life.

Friend, allow me to shed some perspective. You just took two steps forward. And then one step back. You are one step beyond where you were before. This is a champion's march. And you are winning. Don't give up! Just because you collapsed backward again does not mean you are not moving forward at all. You are moving forward. Valiantly.

Keep on.
Forward.
Forward.
Forward.

Your steps will reward you.

Walk Away

You had a bad day. Things happened that you are not proud of. Decisions were made that were poor. You acted out of pain. It was ugly. You were ugly.

Okay. So close your eyes. Hold your breath. Do not over-analyze this day.

This is not a good day for diagnosis. Don't insist on thoroughly understanding it. Abandon it. Walk away. Start over.

One fine thing that every 24-hour day offers is the opportunity for a fresh start soon. Tomorrow is a new day. Begin again.

Part 7: Leaning on God

Prayer

What you need most right now is to rediscover your friendship with God. Or discover it for the first time. There is a place of intersection with the eternal that will stretch your current experience into something much more tolerable, perhaps even hopeful, liberating for certain.

This life is a vapor. There is more to life than this life. There is eternal life. In the eternal, there is a brightness that refuses to dim, a sense of purpose that is unmarred, a place of justice that awaits the gavel. In it, there is space to breathe that is not held hostage by the terror of this moment in your life.

Prayer is the experience that will connect you to the eternal. It is the intersection between this life and the next. Prayer, that very thing that you have darted from for months, is the thing that offers the most tangible comfort and resolve. It awaits you with a safe place to discover the eternal.

Prayer is like standing by the ocean. The soul breathes deeper simply for reckoning with something bigger than itself. Towering clamped anxieties become specks of sand under its relentless tide. Prayer is an entity that lives on with force, a force you cannot deny is outside of you.

When you become aware of the eternal, you discover a vastness there that puts things in perspective and diminishes the pain of the moment.

Prayer is the most delightful escape.

It is the escape that carries you straight home.

The Helper

In recent days, you sought all the help you know how to seek and do not feel any better. You exhausted the list of things that *should* help someone like you, and you are still grieving to the point of illness. When you lie flat, you feel relieved. Your heart is so heavy these days that it is work to be upright at all. The boulder of pain you carry seems to be worsening. Nothing is helping.

There is yet hope.
There is a Helper.
The Holy Spirit.

His ability to help is never exhausted.
His creative caregiving is a remarkable gift.
His powerful presence is a boulder-crushing grace.
He is an expert counselor and not the least bit overwhelmed by your needs.

Close your eyes and ask Him for help.

Then step back and be a witness to His work.
He always answers.

Refined in the Fire

You would never have asked for suffering. Despite this, there are beauties emerging in you through it. There is a deep layer of metal in your heart that is being hammered, refined, and polished by pain. This pain is entirely out of your control, far from a friend, and yet it is producing a glory in you that you now get to live from.

Like gold refined in fire, something is happening to your heart that will cause you to radiate above the rest. There is a purity forming in you. Your values are simplifying into a few solid focuses that really matter. Others will be drawn to you because of the brilliance of who you are becoming. Loss will end up giving you a deep and purposeful life that many fight aimlessly to find, and never do.

Even so, you would never have asked for it, not even now.

Questions for God

You have questions for God. I do too. Questions matter. They create a bridge from what you perceive to what you comprehend. They are the string that connects your conscious mind to your conscious being through validating the need to understand.

Understanding is important.
Ask your questions.
Ask them in detail.

When you ask your questions, release them from your heart. Take care not to tie yourself down to them by demanding answers, as you may be stuck there for a long time. Asking a question is not the same as demanding an answer. Questions are there to serve you, not bind you. Release them like birds, not kites. Let them take off into the sky beyond what you can see. Let go of the string.

But do ask.
Your questions matter.
Ask and release.

When Everything Fails

You may feel that everything failed. Prophecies failed; words of knowledge failed; gifts of the Spirit lie by the wayside in the face of something unexpected that violates the power you thought you knew. People failed you, beliefs failed you, hopes are dashed, and dreams were destroyed. Sometimes life as you know it gets flattened.

In the crux of failure, you discover the one thing that never fails: the love of God. When Jesus hung on the cross, He experienced rejection from the Father. The Father turned His face away. This was punishment that you and I deserve. Jesus absorbed it as an innocent man so that we would never have to know this depth of suffering. Separation from the love of God is a suffering that cannot touch you—ever. Rejection from the Father is off-limits in our lives, barred by the blood of Jesus.

The Father's face is always toward you.

His face is always wearing love.

Nothing can separate you from the love of God.

God's love never fails.

When everything fails, it is an opportunity to grow exponentially in the one thing you have left, the love of God. Cling to the anchor of love. Let your belief in what holds power shift and simplify to this one immovable force, the person of God, who is love. He will never leave you. He will never forsake you. He will never turn His eye away from you for a moment. You are seen. You are loved. You will rise again.

> *Love never fails. But where there are prophecies, they will cease; where there are tongues, they will be restrained; where there is knowledge, it will be dismissed. For we know in part and we prophesy in part, but when the perfect comes, the partial passes away.*
>
> *—1 Corinthians 13:8-10, BSB*

Your Role and God's Role

As one who grieves, you are accustomed to being the unsung hero in your own life. It is steadily unfair. And yet you steadily choose the high road, taking the climb required to continue embracing the life you have. In this you carry the responsibility for your own healing, as you learned the hard way that no one is going to carry it for you. Either you pick it up and work with it, or it holds you in stasis.

Receive my praise.

You are so strong.

In this, I want to remind you that there are certain things that you can and cannot accomplish for yourself and others. You can choose to face another day. You cannot write your own redemption story. You can exert courage to embrace new things. You cannot know for certain which new things are needed. You can choose healthy comforts. You cannot comfort yourself like God can comfort you. You can resist building walls in your life. You cannot ensure your own justice. Some things are your role, and other things are God's role. If you carry the pieces that belong to God, they will become a great burden to your soul. You will find them insurmountable. They belong to a deity.

Good news. You have a friend who is a deity. "Insurmountable" in not in His vocabulary. He took responsibility for your healing. He takes His role in your life seriously. What is your role and what is God's role?

You are my defender and protector; I put my hope in your promise.
—Psalm 119:114, GNB

The Lord is my protector; he is my strong fortress. My God is my protection, and with him I am safe. He protects me like a shield; he defends me and keeps me safe.
—Psalm 18:2, GNB

Moving On

One night the wood burns.
The next morning it is a pile of ashes.

What can become of the ashes?
Nothing, except that they are touched by God.
At which point, somehow—beauty. From ashes.

If you keep touching them, they remain ashes.
If you walk away and let God touch them—beauty.

Reminder: your loyalty is not to the ashes; it is to love.
Love calls you forward.
Love keeps moving on.

Loneliness

Finding an escape from loneliness has become as much a burden to you as the loss itself. Loneliness swallows your emotional energy day after day. In your pain you live with this swelling desire for companionship. Partnership in pain mutes its severity. You long for it. Time passes. There is no one who enters in with you.

Just, loneliness.

What if loneliness is not something to escape? What if there is a depth of love and pain that is yours? What if no one else could possibly understand it? What if the pursuit of an escape from it is futile?

People will come along who will ease the loneliness. Thank God for these people. It may be a child who waves to you on a walk, or a greeter at the door of the church. It may be a sibling who reminds you of your life before loss, or a friend who dares to pop in uninvited. But even then, it is not solved. When that person, that wave, that note, that visit ends, you are still left alone with your grief. No one is living in the deep place of your heart with you, except for God.

Loneliness is part of grief. Your loss is your own. It is personal. The bomb hit your life. Your turf. Your family. Your world. As a result, you are the one who is impacted the most. Your heart is alive to a deeper love and pain than most will ever know. In that inner depth, you face an opportunity for intimacy with God that shimmers with glory.

Loneliness can be an invitation into transcendent communion with God.

There is One who knows.

There is One who gets it.

There is One who promises that you are never truly alone.

If you embrace the self-discovery and intimacy with God available in loneliness, in time it will produce a beauty in your soul that will make the world around you fiercely jealous. You will shine. If you can find your home in God, when no one else is home, you will mine a depth of friendship with God that will then be yours for life.

It is unlikely that anyone else will ever move into the wholeness of your grief with you. It is too deep. No one has access to that place in your life except for God. The hope of companionship there is a hamster wheel of disappointment. Some things are impossible to share in their entirety, as they are far too terrible and... wonderful.

Can you accept this?

Can you allow loneliness to lead you to Jesus?

There, find a companion who will never let go.

> *It is the LORD who goes before you.*
> *He will be with you; he will not leave you or forsake you.*
> *Do not fear or be dismayed.*
>
> *—Deuteronomy 31:8, ESV*

Part 8: Embracing Reality

Waiting for Reality to Repent

You are still waiting and hoping for reality to repent and return to what it was or to become what you had hoped. It's that strong internal resistance to stepping into the present-tense moment of your life and accepting it for what it is. It's okay to feel this. Your heart is letting you know that it is having a hard time facing reality, and rightfully so.

It's important to recognize, however, that the gripping of what is behind is also discoloring what is in front of you now. The good of the present cannot be fully experienced without releasing the good of the past. This is true simply because you cannot live in both at the same time. Presence to one is absence to another.

Reality will not repent, but you can.

The past is not bendable, but you are.

You are not stuck because you can change.

Looking for the Exit

Sorrow is pouring out of the sky of your soul like rain that will not stop pounding the ground. You want to find the exit. You are weary of feeling sad. You hold your emotional breath constantly and are losing strength to keep it up. Upon searching for the exit to your sadness, you find none. You ask yourself sincerely, *Is there an exit?* The thought of this grief not relenting is one that weakens your will to live.

You imagine ways to force an exit, but in them the door you see is burning and its handle hot metal. You could force yourself out but you would also get burned, or even burned up along the way. Or you could wait until the heat dies down and that door becomes an invitation rather than a threat. If the exit is not presenting as a safe way out, then it is not a safe time to exit.

Hello, endurance. You can so do this. You will make it. You will be okay. When this time passes, which it surely will, the endurance you are choosing now will forge in you a strength of heart that the whole world longs to achieve. You will have it because you are choosing it now. Do not give up, beloved.

You do not have to endure alone. Find someone to talk to. Give yourself permission to share what you are experiencing with another person, and without apology for its weightiness. Sharing your honest emotional process will require humility. Accept the state of your weakness and talk about it. It is not shameful to do so; it is courageous.

In the sharing of yourself, you will find a release valve that will strengthen your will to endure. You need the strength that comes into the soul through human interaction. Pursue it. Conversation is a living entity that can move you from one place to the next with an authenticity that you cannot accomplish alone.

Healing is not in the exit right now. It's in the entrance of someone into your process.

People Can't Solve This

Don't keep going to people for something they cannot give you. People cannot solve your grief, neither can they validate your pain rightly. You are living with perpetual relational disappointment, and yet you keep going back to the same people with your needs. Stop it. You deserve better.

Your heart deserves a place that has sufficient room for it. That place is in God. He will not cut you off. He will not call you a burden. He will not pretend to be interested and then forget what you just said. You are not relationally homeless. You are a beloved warrior with a unique injury. There is a difference. You cannot keep expecting foot soldiers below your rank, with no medical expertise, to help you heal. You are a hero in your own story who needs to get into the fortress for expert care.

God is your fortress. God is your expert caregiver. You have liberty right now to develop a beautiful dependence on God that will support you for a very long time. Lean into it.

Regrets

You have many regrets. There are things you could have done differently, things you did not say, moments you failed to embrace. Presently there is one regret in particular that you cannot seem to escape. You believe in your heart that your entire experience would somehow be different if only that one moment had happened.

But it did not.

We have an odd way of reaching backward to try to reconcile things that are facing forward. Have you ever noticed that our physical design is facing forward? Our feet face forward; our arms stretch forward; our eyes look forward. We were designed to focus forward and move forward. Walking backward, reaching backward, gazing backward are terribly uncomfortable, and with good reason: it is terribly disheartening for the soul. Holding regrets holds you back.

You could not have known what was coming, and neither could you have prepared any better for it. You did your best. Regrets are futile attempts to re-create time passed. The ironic thing is that regret actually kills time. Gratitude lengthens time. The best way to redeem what is behind you is to thread the entire thing with the lace of gratitude.

Let go of regrets.

You cannot change the past.

It's futile work.

Self-perception

Your self-perception is that you are covered in ashes. Your sense of personal dignity is tainted by the soot of your experience. You feel weak, exposed, incapable, and somehow distorted. You see yourself as broken.

Your self-perception is wrong. Your dignity is as strong as it has ever been as you courageously take this strenuous hike in life. You are covered in beauty that radiates from a heart reflecting the heart of Christ. You are strong, hidden, capable, and brilliant. You are nothing short of magnificent.

How will you come to see yourself rightly? You may discover it on your own. And you may not. However, others will see it in you.

Let others encourage you. Let their admiration penetrate your pain and restore your personal sense of dignity.

When they say, "You are strong," do not spit it out.

When they say, "You are beautiful," pause.

When they say, "You are a hero," at least consider it.

Let the gentle encouragement of others blow the ashes off your self-perception so that you can see yourself rightly in time. Look again. See? You are a beautiful and courageous soul that is shining with strength and dignity, even in your pain.

Moving Out of Blame

People say they care about you. They say that the way they are caring for you right now is by "giving you space." These people do not understand grief. Those who grieve need companionship, presence, comfort, and commitment in and through their raw experience of pain. Absence and abandonment are not care for the grieving.

Despite this, some people have convinced themselves that what you need is for them to be distant. This is their way to avoid the personal cost of presence with you, while maneuvering verbally that they are not divorcing their care for you. Other people choose presence and are terrible at it. It seems that they own a horn that is specifically designed to blow unpleasant noises into your tender grief journey.

There are so many people standing around the periphery of your life, waiting for you to get better, unwilling to help you get there as it would cost them something. And it would. Standing with the injured costs something.

Mature friends dare to be with you when you are hurting, and not just wait on the sidelines until it's all over. It is odd but people convince themselves that some magical relational proximity will reappear with you after defending relational absence through the entire process. Friendship doesn't, and won't, work that way.

Admit that you are hurt. Decide if you want to tell the person or not. There is no right or wrong route here, but you must take responsibility for yourself and not land in blame of others. Move out on blame. Take responsibility for your experience of this friendship and decide what the right course of action is for you, whether to engage or walk away.

Closure

Closure is a mysterious thing. It cannot be bought or traded. It cannot be forced or found by prescription. It is something you feel that you need but cannot find your way to through willpower. People talk about it like it is a common experience, as if you can get to it simply, through automatic living. I question if it is real, and how alive those people are who say they have it.

There is only one thing I have found that provides real closure, and that is the voice of God.

The ability to open or close something is a creative power that comes from eternity. Hearing God's voice on a matter can settle it. Memories can heal, longings subside, pain disappear, and the need for justice can find a new home. There is a creative power in the voice of God that can bring closure.

Outside of that, I question whether closure of any kind exists.

Within it, I know it does.

Does This Last Forever?

No, and yes.

The space of loss you hold will be there for life. What fills it, your experience of grief, will change. Grief will not always define you or even look like it does right now. It will transform, retreat, disappear, and then be around for visits. By that time, it will have metamorphosed from ashes to beauty. The visits will be welcome, like an old friend.

The ability to grieve is now yours for life. That, my friend, is a precious gift. God is beautiful, especially in darkness. You now get to know that, one holy day at a time.

Part 9: Releasing Your Grip

Letting Your Heart Go Free

"Nothing but blue skies."

Can I trust this?

Some things are going well now for you, but it feels impossible to expect it or trust it. Emotional pain left its mark on your brain. You know too much. Innocent expectations are long lost in the dust of past experiences. You can imagine always being like this, forever marred by the shadows of loss, with an undercurrent of expecting the worst just in case you find yourself there again. My question for you is, do you believe that you can change?

The change I allude to is not about your circumstances; it's about your heart. It's about whether or not you can recover from tragedy to the point of childlike hope again. If you can, would you allow it? "No guarantees," you tell me. "I could be burned again."

I choose to challenge you because I know you can take it.

What good are guarantees anyway? That's part of what you know too much of. Guarantees collapse at times, unapologetically. Since they are so unreliable, why are you allowing them to dictate what you can and cannot enjoy right now? You are serving self-protection and it is far less dependable than you think. Why pay the cost of living disengaged from your own life for something you cannot trust?

There is no guarantee that your life will brighten.

But there is also no guarantee that it will not.

When your life starts brightening outside,

For God's sake, let it brighten inside.

Let your heart go free.

Otherwise, you are now holding yourself hostage. That's a much different scenario than when grief held you. Enough with the hostage. Enough with the slavery to pain. Enough with the scars of the past. Let yourself go. Maybe you will find out that you are actually quite good at living free from all of this. It's worth checking.

When Grief Resigns

As those who grieve, we become committed to grief. It becomes a companion, a validator of our journey, a safe place to express our hearts. There comes a time when we have the opportunity to part ways with it as a primary friend. It will always be part of our lives, but eventually it wants to change shape.

Before you were acquainted with grief, you would assume such an offer would be grabbed and swallowed. Now, however, you find yourself faced with a dilemma. Grief is a safe place for your heart, and that may be something you never had before grief had you. If it goes, what will become of you? Who will know you? Only God knows. And you will miss grief if you let it go—as odd as that sounds. But be forewarned that grief does not remain kind when it stays too long.

There is a time and season for every activity under heaven. You have spent a long time in this activity of grief. The season is now changing around you. You have to decide whether you will let the season change within you.

From the outside looking in, joy does not feel safe, hope does not feel safe, goodness does not feel safe, and innocent expectations on life definitely do not feel safe. Your friendship with grief hinders you from blindly entering any of these things from the heart.

Don't let your assumptions from the outside looking in cause you to forget that you are actually on the inside looking out. You were locked up in the wilderness of grief for a long time. If grief is offering you its resignation, it is time for you to step out of the darkness and back into the light. Don't be found running late. You worked hard for this release. It is your reward. Take it.

Your loss will always be with you, but the grief that expresses it will change.

You were made for more than grief, friend.
At your heart of hearts, you know this is true.
There is more for you than sorrow.
More than overcoming disappointment.
More than faithfulness through pain.

Will the light hurt?
Probably.

Will you be safe?
Probably not.

Will you be happy?
Oh, so much happier.

And you will no longer be stuck at war.
At last, a sojourner coming to rest.
The battle is over.
Come home.

A Lot to Unlearn

There is a lot to unlearn when you transition from full-time grieving. To name a few:

>You are invisible.
>You are unknown.
>You are incapable of hoping.
>Your future looks bleak.
>Your story feels over.

These are beliefs in grief that are no longer true when the grief cloud dissipates. Define for yourself what these frames are that need to be replaced and what the replacement is. For example:

>You are not invisible anymore.
>You are capable of hoping now.
>Your future is bright.
>Your story is not over.

Can you embrace these swaps? Unlearn a few things? It will serve you well as you continue to put one foot in front of the other in this process. Each exchanged belief is liberty from a specific resistance to the life that calls you onward.

>Make a list of things that you need to unlearn.
>Make a list of things you now need to relearn.
>Meditate on both, on purpose.

The Imprint of Loss

Loss changed you. The imprint of it is with you, even when grief moves out, or you move out on grief. You are a new shape. That change in you is not reversible, but neither is it undesirable. It is actually quite remarkable, and beautiful.

The imprint of loss is a sacred space, a holy place within that will long host for you the most precious moments in life. You can spot someone with loss because their love runs very deep. They care about what matters. Their inner beauty is otherworldly. They are not afraid to look people square in the eye.

I believe the scars of loss can heal, the heart that was empty can refill, the spirit that was broken can be mended, and the shadows of sorrow can be removed. I don't believe that we ever lose the imprint of loss. It becomes part of our glorious wholeness through Christ. I don't believe that we need or want to lose it if we consider what it has given to us and the world around us. God blots out sin, not stories. Your story is a healing force for you and others. God's redemptive work takes the raw materials of what exists and does not erase them but rather transforms them for a noble use.

May the holiness of your suffering always feed you, give you favor, and cause you to shine without retreat. May the imprint of your loss undergird your life experience with gold, and therein cause you to be deeply satisfied with all that is not lost.

From one friend to another, I spot your imprint, and you don't need to fear losing it. It's in you; it's part of your shape now. Your being holds a sacred glory forged in suffering that will not die. Do not fear moving on. What you treasure will always be with you. Always.

Part 10: Redemption Bells

Early Stages

I am convinced that our lives will look different when we see them at last, start to finish, from an eternal perspective. Part of that difference will be our exploding understanding of redemption and justice.

That said, redemption is not stuck in the afterlife. It is eternal, which means that it is already present in some way. It is touching us, even now. There is something about our faith in it, ability to feel it, keen ear for its emergence that activates another layer of healing for those who grieve. Some choose never to ascend to it. They level off in a different stage of grief and call redemption something else. I believe that redemption is a part of grief and holds its offering freely to all who grieve.

There are times when the bells of redemption ring in our lives and we would do well to learn how to identify them, to stop, listen, and internalize what the sound points toward, and what it all means for us.

At the time of this writing, I am in the early stages of exploring this topic in the context of my own story. Grief has been the primary emotion and lens for my life for over a decade. May that encourage those who feel pressured by the "you will get over this in a year" noise. May it also hold no one from moving on in a year or less if you possess that grace. The point is that only now am I able to approach this topic from the heart. It takes time to see it, but at some point, your grief will offer you this ascension.

I anticipate that I will always view myself in the "early stages" of the topic of redemption until I am in the "later stages" on the shores of eternity being ambushed by it. Find me there! Until then, I am an explorer whom God is calling forward. I am uncertain how much of my perspective will require repentance later, and yet I'm certain that this realm of truth holds a critical piece of healing for the brokenhearted. We must explore it.

Redemption is part of grief, the best part.

Trusting God's Artistry

When you look at the blotches in your own story from an earthly perspective, it's tempting to start filling in the empty spaces of your narrative yourself with what you think should be there. You are convinced that if you were God, you would know exactly how to fix this sorrowful mess. You would erase what is there and create something perfect. You think you know what you want and need. You think you know what "perfect" would look like.

But do you?
Do I?

We have no idea how much we rob ourselves when we distrust God's artistry in our lives. His overlay is far beyond what you and I could ever come up with for our own stories. It's a sad day when we use up His ink space for our own redemptive guesses.

Can you trust Him?

Your divine redemption blueprint is being overlaid onto your narrative, even now. Its perfection is beyond your comprehension. It will transform your life experience with touches of divine beauty. Yours is a powerful and exquisite story. Wait until you see what He is doing. When you step back and see it at last, you will find yourself glorified in it, even though He deserves all the glory.

A Call out of Apathetic Hope

Job was a man who suffered severely. A marathon of losses attacked his life. One loss hit, then another, then another. Each area of his life was hit by disaster, tragedy, and his heart was tested through it all. I do not understand his story, and honestly, I do not like it. It's in the Bible, however, and for a reason.

One reason that I can identify clearly is that this is a man who suffered multiple losses, as many of us do. His strength of heart does a good amount of wreckage to our self-pity cycles and calls you and me to the high road, even in the midst of great suffering.

Job's words about the "Redeemer" are pillars to countless believers. For centuries, weary souls have caught his declaration and allowed it to become their song of strength. When Job was hit with injustice, this is what came out of him:

> *But I know that my Redeemer lives,*
> *and in the end He will stand upon the earth.*
> *Even after my skin has been destroyed,*
> *yet in my flesh I will see God.*
> *I will see Him for myself;*
> *my eyes will behold Him,*
> *and not as a stranger.*
> *How my heart yearns within me!*
>
> —*Job 19:25-27, BSB*

When I thought about this passage recently, I made this assumption: There is no way that he made that declaration until he knew for certain that it was true. These verses must have been written after God restored all that he lost.

But when I looked it up, I found that I was wrong. This declaration was made in the middle of his tragedy. Job did not wait until the Redeemer performed to declare in confidence that He would. Talk about a heart that is strong in the Lord!

It is easy for me to sit and wait for God to prove Himself as a redeemer. I can sit back in apathetic hope and say, "I will celebrate who You are when I see it." I can easily exhort you, as my beloved friends who are grieving, to not give up "hope" but wait and watch to see what God will do, wait for Him to prove Himself.

But redemption is calling us to something higher than this apathetic hope of "If it happens, it happens." Redemption is calling us to believe in God, that He is who He says He is. Redemption is giving us a prized opportunity to become strong in heart as it relates to our relationship with God.

Before we see it.
Before it touches us.
Before we are convinced of its presence.

Can you and I say,

"I know.
That my redeemer lives.
And that He will stand on the earth.
And make this right for me."

This requires faith.
Will you believe?

Redeemer God

Redemption is a deep, thorough work of grace that contains an astounding amount of goodness. It is so encompassing that it exceeds the capacity of any human being to produce it. It can only be fully performed by God. It is a divine ability to create something otherworldly that intertwines with this world.

Redemption is part of God's personality, His nature, His being. It flows from Him in force like water from a water fountain, pressed whenever someone dares to trust Him with that role. Performing redemption is one of the brilliant acts of God. Stand back and watch Him work.

Watch.

Wait.

Gasp.

Cheer.

There is One who is fully capable of this thing we call "redemption" and He wants each of us to take deep delight in His solo ability to redeem something well. He is honestly overqualified for the needs of our stories, but like an expert who loves to serve those in need, He is willing to engage in this role for us. For me. For you. Redemption is part of the personality of God. You can no sooner strip someone of their personality then remove this attribute from the nature of God.

He is a redeemer.

It is who He is.

Until Your Heart Is Full Again

People will look at circumstances in your life—occurrences, experiences, changes—and call it "redemption." They will tell you, "That is redemption for what you went through." Most of the time, their estimation is shallow and inaccurate. It diminishes your loss to a replaceable earthly object.

True redemption does not further detract from your sense of loss. It understands the eternal weight of how you were robbed and the importance of your loss as you experienced it. It is not a replacement theory. When redemption comes, it transforms your loss into a newfound identity. It doesn't hurt; it heals.

For some reason, those with loss are sometimes expected to treat all positive experiences in life as a "special gift" or "redemption" when these things are normal in the lives of others and not categorized as such by a long shot. I find this problematic, as I do not believe redemption creates a hierarchy to the detriment of the grieving. I think redemption levels hierarchy into an equal opportunity of the goodness of God by all, like what Jesus came and performed with His brief beautiful life.

What appears like a blessing to others may amplify your loss. A "fresh start" may expose the depth of your pain. What someone else thinks will make you happy may in fact be salt on the wound of your loss. Your heart knows its own loss, and your heart will know when that loss loses its sting. It will likely not be what others expect that causes the sting to dissipate. But it will be deeply personal and meaningful to you.

The external perspectives on your redemption can be disturbing and cause you to settle prematurely on what is possible for the grieving. I recommend you disregard any claim of redemption for your story that causes you to hurt inside, feel robbed, or corners you as an unprivileged person on planet Earth. These outcomes are not God's heart for you, and they are not full redemption.

Redemption is not fulfilled until your heart is full again.

It is yours to identify.

When Redemption Comes

Redemption is so big that when it buds you find that it was budding the entire time, like a map that courageously overlays the entire narrative from beginning to end. It is not event focused. It encompasses more of your life than you even had on the map. It will shock you with a heavenly measure of goodness. It will not be a logical or rational repayment. It will not be the same size, shape, color, or purpose as the loss. It will be broader than any replacement scenario you imagined.

You will know when redemption has come because "then you will look and be radiant, your heart will throb and swell with joy" (Isaiah 60:5, NIV). It is not a doing experience; it is a discovery that you have become something, someone who is radiant and with a full heart. Redemption is not about being "paid back." It is about being loved, without any spot left untouched. It is about something so good that your heart has to swell to make room for it.

You will know redemption is touching down because you will become the sign of its presence. You yourself will become a shiny piece of redemption on the earth.

And it will happen.

Even the most tarnished medal can find a fresh shine.

Hope, dear heart.

Justice

You will rob yourself if you take on the role of redeemer in your own life. If you believe that justice is in your own hands and it is somehow courageous for you to go and assure it, your need for justice will likely become a toxin that controls your life, even subconsciously. I shudder when people make statements like, "This is to make the enemy pay for that." In my opinion, they are holding in that statement a job description that belongs to God: Judge.

Put the gavel down.
Let go.

Redemption is a role for God. It takes divine capacity that you don't have. If you assume it, you will lose the space inside for Him to fill. You have a decision to make whether you are going to pursue your own justice or give that role to God. Friend, He will not disappoint you.

The enemy will pay in full for what he destroyed in my life. May I be found with this anthem: "Jesus is my advocate. Let Him speak for me."

The Value of Time

Immediate.
Shortcut.
Cheap.
Expedited.
Speedy.
Quick.
Fast.
Instant.
Overnight.
Now. Now. Now.

It's hard to understand why redemption does not find a home in any of these words. I would be surprised if anyone defined their redemption experience using these descriptors. *But why? If someone has the power to fix this (e.g., God), then why is it not being fixed right now?*

I propose that redemption is actually immediately and presently at work in our lives. The intrusion of it into our conscious stories takes time. The time, in my opinion, speaks to the value, stability, and dependability of what it is becoming for and with us. It is a grace to us.

If a building of grandiose architecture that took twenty years to build makes a tragic collapse and a new one appears overnight, would you trust the new structure as equally valuable? If you order a steak dinner at a diner and it comes out ten seconds later, do you trust it? If an elevator breaks to the injury of people and a technician assures you five minutes later that it is all fixed, would you trust it?

God can do anything He wants to, as fast as He wants to. God is interested in more than flaunting His abilities. He is interested in restoring us personally in our hearts and our capacity. He is interested in assuring that we come out rich from our losses, not just in appearance, but with a deep gut-level-honest, heart-pulsing experience.

I believe that we, friends, are the reason that redemption takes time. Time is a grace for our heart to gain the capacity it needs not to be destroyed by the coming gifts but rather to be an active participant in and with them. The stretching of time is for our benefit. None of the time is sterile or wasted. It is all purposeful to the outcomes God intends to bring forward for us.

The gratitude that this time is building in you now will serve you for life. The appreciation for what matters is stabilizing your spirit. Your heart is being transformed by love that costs something, and that is worth more than any expedited blessing. Trust God with the timing of redemption. As the psalmist said,

> *I lift my eyes to You, the One enthroned in heaven.*
> *As the eyes of servants look to the hand of their master…*
> *so our eyes are on the LORD our God until He shows us mercy.*
> —*Psalm 123:1-2, BSB*

Redemption is a deeply personal process that can take years to unfold.

"Now!" would be a cheap version of what we will get later. The wait is not for nothing; it is part of the momentum He is building so that you and I gain more. Redemption does not pair well with immediate gratification; it has a preemptive loyalty to lifelong rewards. Time is stretching so that you and I win in all things. God is not absent, apathetic, lazy, or distant. He is making decisions about the timing of your redemption experience that is purely for your benefit.

Simply put, you landed in a marathon. The prize doesn't come if you cut out at mile 7. You are going to win this marathon and not quit. The passing of time that you feel is crawling is about God delicately assuring all the pieces are present for you to come in first place in your own story and get the strong finish you deserve.

That's what the time factor is about.

It's about and for you.

Extensions into Eternity

The foundation of God's throne is righteousness and justice. I believe this means that there is nothing that will escape His redemptive power in our lives. Some of this experience is held in eternity, and that makes some of us mad. But should it? Is it so awful to have the best of our lives preserved in a place where it will never end? A place where nothing can rob us of it?

> *Do not store up for yourselves treasures on earth, where moths and vermin destroy, and where thieves break in and steal. But store up for yourselves treasures in heaven, where moths and vermin do not destroy, and where thieves do not break in and steal. For where your treasure is, there your heart will be also.*
>
> *—Matthew 6:19-21, NIV*

Those who are grieving in this life have a lot to look forward to in eternity.

Some of God's redemption for you will land in your lifetime. It will feel like a gold thread shooting through the fragments of your life and pulling them together into a purposeful and unified existence. It will cause your view of loss to change, and you will understand it oddly as gain, not necessarily good, but gain.

Other parts of God's redemption for you will not land with you now but are landing already for you in eternity. There is a time beyond this one that holds even greater promise for your story. In eternity, we will all get to see your shining life, making sense from beginning to end. The divine wisdom of it all will make us gasp repeatedly until we fall over tickled with delight at how much we did not perceive about the intentional love of our Father.

You will stand before an unveiled God who will present you with redemption for your life because of the sacrifice of Jesus for you. Every tear fallen in faithfulness holds a reward in that realm. I am convinced of this. No one knows what your full redemption is going to look like except the King of Redemption Himself, and trust me, He is not done with your story.

It stretches on, far beyond where you sit today.

All things will be made right.

All things. All.

Redemption.

It's who He is.

We will know it fully,

When we fully know Him.

The Bells of Redemption

When I was a child, I had an unusual interest in church bells. Something about the cathedral tower and the sound that would bellow from it unannounced stirred my heart. My father is a musician with a keen ear. He noticed how church bells stopped me in my tracks as a little girl. I can remember him observing me frozen on the street. He knew exactly what I was doing. I was listening.

"Can you tell, Katie, if that is a real or artificial sound?" Initially I could not, and so he taught me. We worked together on training my ear. Over time, I could clearly identify the real bells.

My family spent some time traveling in Russia. I was eight years old at the time. It was there that my dad and I bonded further in this experience of sound. The orthodox cathedral bells rang often and I was found transfixed by them—listening with a keen ear and attentive heart. Almost every church bell we heard on that trip was a real sound. My tolerance for artificial sound deteriorated as a child. I fell in love with the ageless ringing of these metal wonders.

I can remember stopping in the street on that trip as if gold were falling from the sky into my lap. My dad would bend down to my level and we would listen together quietly until the last bell's resonance faded. Then we would make a judgment call on the sound: real or fake?

In those moments of listening, I remember hoping that the ballad of bells would never end, somehow caught in a magical moment of sound, outdoors, on the street. I recall the disappointment when artificial bells were exposed, and the way my attention would drain before their performance was over. I remember looking up at silent church bells encased in towers and wondering why they were sitting there lifeless for so long. I wondered if anyone pulled their strings anymore. If not, what a waste of beauty. Bells should not remain mute for long.

The sound of church bells became one of my favorite experiences, a highlight of that trip to Russia, and an ongoing interest. Perhaps I like them because I love sound but am also an active and impatient person. The beauty of bells arrests me for a moment and then lets me scurry onward. Maybe it is the interruption itself that I love, something in the sky calling my attention away. Perhaps my dad's bright eyes on the topic of sound made me want to find for myself what brightened them. Or maybe the sound of church bells holds some kind of eternal significance that will long hold weight in my own story.

Today I find this latest explanation most likely.

Maybe the sound of bells is prophetic.
Maybe there are bells waiting for their moment to sound.
Maybe their sound is connected to the sound of redemption.
Maybe my story and yours solicits the sound of redemption.

When I think of redemption, I think of the ringing of eternal bells. I can imagine cathedral towers all over the realm of eternity whose strings hold a connection to each of our stories. I can see it with the eyes of my heart—the bells of redemption, pinned into the sky with our names attached.

These bells will not remain quiet forever. They will ring. A time will come when our Redeemer will pull on the strings of our stories so hard, swinging back and forth as some do, to make the metal sing—with an alarming confidence—this timeless anthem:

> *"Now the dwelling place of God is with man, and He will live with them. They will be His people, and God Himself will be with them and be their God. He will wipe every tear from their eyes."*

And there will be—

No more death,
or mourning,
or crying,
or pain,
for the old order of things has passed away.

He who was seated on the throne said, "I am making everything new!"

Then he said, "Write this down, for these words are trustworthy and true.

—Revelation 21:3-5, NIV

I believe that this anthem is already being sung over your story. Some of it wants to touch you now, and some is reserved for later. It will all touch you in time.

The bells of redemption will ring.
The bells of justice will ring.
Destruction will face its end.
In that, your story will bloom into full redemption.

…put your hope in the LORD, for with the LORD is unfailing love and with him is full redemption.

—Psalm 130:7, NIV

Redemption is a promise.
It is real.
As real as a bell.
It's a special gift—
For the grieving.

Here it comes!

THANK YOU

I hold the deepest respect for those who grieve.
You are my heroes, the great champions of our earth.
Thank you for not giving up.
Thank you for facing another day.
Thank you for engaging with these letters.
And thank you for letting your pain birth deeper love in our world.

The bells of redemption will ring!
Together, let's listen!
Forever.

You are done with this book.
Good for you!

Go!
Run away, friend.
Run far, far away.

Chase the light that has somehow found you. Let it swallow you whole. Accept the kisses of sunlight. Let the wind push you onward. Don't hang back here with us. Be released to reside outside of grief.

These pages will remain present if you ever need to revisit them, and they also accept the trash with a cheer if that's where they now belong in your life.

Go on!
Run!

Love,
Katie Luse

TELL YOUR STORY

Your story holds power. You already know that it is precious, but you may not know the power it holds for others. Far too often we hold our stories so closely that they never find the wind and wings to propel them into the heights where they belong. Our stories become like kites being dragged along the ground without any wind. They long for freedom but will not find it unless we dare to hold them up high and let them go.

Over the last ten years, I stood on countless stages and broke open my story. I shared about my grief in meetings, with friends, in one-on-ones. I wrote about it and published it. I took the holy trail of grief within and gave it away. I did it in places where it was popular and unpopular, celebrated and despised, public and hidden. I did this not because of some twisted impulse or self-fulfilling need. I gave my story away out of love for God. I did it because I believe that in the hands of God, my ashes can be transformed into beauty. Outside of myself, my story is finding a broadening purpose. Yours will too.

I've studied miracles of multiplication and found that most often they are catalyzed by someone who is giving away all that they have. Giving it all seems to send a signal that more is needed, that there is room for more. Right there, the more begins. As long as we are gripping our stories, they will do nothing more than spoil and occupy the space for new things in our lives. When we find a way to give our stories away, they feed others and make room in our lives for more.

Friend, can you give your story away? Can you face it long enough to discover that it is bread for another? How can you express what you have come to know? Are you considering writing your story? Are you considering going there the next time you share or speak? Please do. You must.

The hard-earned words of wisdom and authority that are found in the grieving are bread for a starving world. If you and I lift our voices to give away what we have, multitudes will be sustained through their own seasons of grief.

Value your trail; become a guide.

Share your story; you must.

For more information and book orders visit:

www.katieluse.com

~

Other books by Katie & Mitch Luse:

Ruby Joy, Finding Gems in Darkness (Katie Luse)

The 5:25 Call, God's Design for Husbands (Mitch Luse)

Printed in France by Amazon
Brétigny-sur-Orge, FR

13226982R00089